What Others Have to Say about This Book

"There are people that you meet in life that have special gifts and callings. Having known Dr. Rick Barrett for a while, I came to realize he is that rare person that possesses both. He was called to be a Chiropractor so that through the healing touch of Chiropractic, he can see the lives of people change and through the gift of writing, he can touch the very heart and soul of mankind.

I consider his new book, *Healed by Morning*, a masterpiece. If after reading this book, you are not completely on focus and have a purpose for life then read the book again. I read this book when I was going through a very desperate time in my life and I can truthfully say this book helped save my life. Thank you, Dr. Barrett, for using that special gift God gave you and don't ever quit."

Dr. Darrell Petrey

"Wow! A truly inspiring, touching, moving, and practical book. There were moments when I nearly cried. Get this for yourself and as gifts for friends. It is a priceless work!"

Joe Vitale
Author of "Spiritual Marketing"

"Dr. Barrett has a powerful message for us all in a great time of need. We can heal ourselves and he helps to light the way."

Vickie Alleman
Health Care Marketing Consultant

"I am blown away by this book! I believe that it is going to bring much healing. This is one of the best things I have ever read. It is that good! I believe that it is inspired by God!"

Pat Kushnir
Health and Nutrition Consultant

"Dr. Barrett is truly the kind of holistic healing practitioner that the world needs during these chaotic times. This holistic philosophy is reflected in all of his healing endeavors—as an author, a seminar presenter, a volunteer service provider for the underprivileged and as a one-on-one practitioner with his patients and colleagues. It is rare that I have come across a wellness professional like Dr. Barrett who truly understands how the body, emotions, mind and spirit are intimately connected, and through this understanding, how to treat illness and promote wellness in such a way which honors this integration resulting in efficient and effective outcomes. In this book, Dr. Barrett has soared to new heights in offering a simplified guidebook to holistic health and well-being. I highly recommend this book to anyone who genuinely is ready to experience a level of health and happiness that others only dream of achieving."

Susan Marshall, President
Center for Total Wellness

"I was privileged to read a "rough" copy of Dr. Barrett's book and was touched by his desire to offer hope to those plagued by pain that there are practical ways to manage it by chiropractic. His desire to help others is a thread which runs throughout his text."

"Healing is a complex process, but encouragement to seek it from a mentor such as Dr. Barrett can be an exciting adventure. Believing oneself worthy to be healed was a message Jesus gave to those He touched and healed. Dr. Barrett's care for patients' recoveries is contagious; His positive comments belie his faith in the healing process as well as an individual's duty to participate in his/her own healing."

"In addition to expert manipulation of the spine, his knowledge of nutrition and its impact of health is a bonus. Upon his recommendation of certain herbal remedies, including herbal tea and fiber, my overall health has improved. Because I believe God created us, it seems a caring Creator also gave us plants, which are compatible with our bodies' healing systems. He enables patients to practice self-care to maintain optimum health."

Healed by Morning symbolizes the beginning step essential to good health, a favorable attitude. My hope is that this book will have a life changing impact on its readers."

Barbara Boothe Loyd
Artist

"Dr. Barrett's passion for helping people take responsibility for their health, physically, mentally, and spiritually, is clear. He truly believes in his calling and shares that belief in this book."

Doug Earle
YMCA Executive Director

DR. R. F. BARRETT

Dream Weaver Press, Sugar Land, Texas

This book is intended to create inspiration in the reader, to give guidance and support a natural path to healing. It is meant to be thought provoking and motivate the reader to become educated, take their own journey and decide what is the correct form of healing for them. Every attempt has been made to make the content of this book accurate.

However, errors may occur. The philosophy and opinions of the author do not necessarily reflect the philosophy and opinions of other natural healers or biblical scholars.

The author and publisher shall not be responsible to any person or entity in regards to any damages, losses, whether real or alleged from the information contained in this book.

Healed by Morning: Messages from God For the 21st Century On Herbs, Natural Healing, and Drugs

By Dr. R. F. Barrett

Published by: Dream Weaver Press
Sugar Land, Texas
1-866-222-4325

Manufactured in the United States of America
ISBN: 0-9705431-0-7

Footnote: Dexidrine, Adderall, Cylert, Syban, Luvox, Zoloft, Ritalin, Prozac, Tylenol, and Advil, are registered trademarks.

Contents

Dedication

This book is dedicated to my mother Who years before it became popular, embarked on a journey in pursuit of natural healing. She had the courage to stand tall and fast against a storm of criticism and ignorance. Also, to all of you who are not afraid of shedding light on the darkness, by empowering yourselves and others, to heal naturally.

Acknowledgments

The Gift...Giving Thanks

As I contemplate the journey I have taken to complete this book, I reflect on all the thanks I must give. One thank you that decidedly must be first is—to God. Thank you for the creation of this book and allowing me to be one of the messengers, as I feel that it was truly a gift to me. It was only by His grace that this book exists at all. But not only is it a gift to me, but a gift to every man, woman, and child that will read it, benefit from it and be changed by it.

Special thanks to Mary, the mother of Jesus, and of us all. Praying the rosary gave me special peace and strength to finish this book.

I never walked alone on this journey as Jesus guided my way. Just as the words from the passage, "Footprints", says, "My precious child, I love you and I would never leave you. During your times of trial and suffering, when you see only one set of footprints, it was then that I carried you." I can truly say there were numerous times when I felt that I was surely being carried.

I do not write these words casually, as I have always been a person who guards his inner most feelings and thoughts closely. It can be a risk to profess your faith, even to the faithful. My relationship with God has always been a personal one. So by writing these words, it is to remain honest with God and profess what is in my heart. This book would not exist if God had not wished it to.

Every written word, I have thought and believed in my heart and to the depths of every living cell of my body. Therefore, I am compelled to add permanence to my thoughts by casting them to paper, which brings life to them for all eternity.

Other thanks go to my mother, Vlasta, and father, Joe. Both of whom have given me strength, guidance and wisdom. Not only now, but through all the years. "Healed by Morning" is a tribute to their individual and collective strengths that are manifested in me. Without their love and religious character, my spirit would not exist as it does. Therefore, this book would never have been created. Gratitude and love also go out to my sister, Kathy, and brother, Ken, additional sources of strength, and guidance throughout my life. Growing up in a loving family environment with them, contributed to the formation of my being.

Deep love and appreciation to my beloved, Mary, who spent countless hours assisting me during the forging of this book. Not only did she physically aid in the production of the book, but also she was a constant source of encouragement and moral support, especially during times of difficulty and doubt when my energy was low. Truly she stood with me, making the vision a reality and providing me with prayerful support.

To Joe Vitale who has been a friend and mentor. He

has listened to my ideas and has been a source of encouragement and inspiration. His words uplift me and provide renewed enthusiasm each time I have needed it. Upon reading my rough draft, Joe apparently saw beyond its roughness to write me a note saying, "Finish it! I love it! This is your best book yet. It can change lives!"

To my wonderful friend, Marian, who is a joy to be in the same space with. Another recipient of an early draft. Her sheer enjoyment and words of praise were enough to know this book could touch lives. Thanks for your effusive personality and support.

To my good friend, Patty Hoelker, who provided me with her beautiful poem, "He Touches".

To all who have read the manuscripts, offered words of love, support and encouragement, and to all who have allowed me to reproduce your testimonies, I thank you. Each one of you has added to the creation of this work. Each one of you are now captured in time immortal and give this book life.

Thank you!

Introduction

There are so many powerful stories told about the success of individuals through the power of God's intervention, the strength that comes from prayer, and the hope given from reaching people. These stories come from small entrepreneurs to powerful national and international figures. People preach about it. Others such as Mark Victor Hanson write books about it, like "Chicken Soup for the Christian Soul". The one thing they have in common is the utmost unshakable faith in a higher power—in God.

In this book, what I have worked to accomplish is not just to tell more stories, although, they can be wonderfully uplifting, but to reach down into God's word. I have extracted passages and quotes from the Bible to lend support, give courage, and let you know that what you are feeling and what you are doing is by His command with His blessing.

"Commit to the Lord whatever you do, and your plans will succeed."

-Proverbs 16:3

Preface

What is our responsibility to our fellow man? The Veda—ancient sacred writings of the Hindus, the Dharma of Asia, Tao of China, Talmud of the Jews, the Old and New Testaments of the Bible; what do they all have in common?

All cultures and religions of the planet hold ideals that human beings must care for one another and that our lives are a special gift. Not to be taken lightly, life should be treasured and enhanced through natural means; not desecrated, defiled and destroyed. We are clearly each other's keepers and if we keep each other well, we will be rewarded beyond our expectations. These ancient and universal principals are timeless. Today, philosophers, scholars, heads of churches, heads of countries, and human rights activists, all echo these basic premises.

Christianity clearly promotes this. When Jesus was asked what the greatest commandment was he replied,

"Love the Lord your God with all your heart and with all your soul and with all your mind and with all your strength. The second is this, love your neighbor as yourself".

-Mark 12:30-31

Jesus said love and honor God above everything, but next love your neighbor the same way you would love yourself! Through this powerful message, he places caring for our neighbors next to God. What incredible significance! Jesus said the second greatest commandment is to love your neighbor as yourself!

How better to show our love for one another than to provide for their health, and healing? Helping one another to heal naturally certainly fulfills loving our neighbor. The second most important commandment!

It is of no matter whether you are a Christian, Jew, Muslim, Buddhist, Scientologist, or a spiritual seeker not tied to any one denomination. The concepts of Jesus and others, prophets and visionaries who focus on the goodness of the human spirit, the essence of man, all share the same basic truth, which can be universally applied.

"God has many names though he is only one being".

-Aristotle

I don't profess to be a biblical scholar. There are scores of individuals who are more learned and better suited to speak with authority on the Bible. Each person reads and is free to ponder on the words, use his God given free will and glean his own wisdom from the words. Any written word is a thought and as such, can be interpreted freely and differently by each individual. What is contained in this book are quotes, passages, and ideas extracted from the Bible and other sources. They are my thoughts and interpretations.

I hope that you find this book inspiring and uplifting; it aids you in your quest for health and your pursuit of sharing natural healing with others.

This book is for those who are involved and interested in alternative health care, whether you are a professional or a consumer. Maybe you are a chiropractor, naturopath, herbologist, massage therapist, acupuncturist, a medical doctor who is turning to alternative approaches or a health food storeowner. Maybe you use natural products yourself and influence your family to use them. Perhaps you sell herbs and nutritional supplements through a multilevel marketing company. This is for you also, the producers, sellers, and distributors of natural health products, specifically herbs and nutritional supplements. This book is about giving you guidance and inspirational support, to speak to the part of you that innately knows there is a greater good. Though money may be a direct factor in your involvement with nutritional products, there is a greater and more divine purpose for your business, and if that is satisfied, then all things can be realized. There are no limits!

I want you to learn how to be "Healed by Morning", why it is possible and how to share this wisdom with others. This book is meant to serve those of you who have chosen to serve mankind by delivering better health.

"For even the son of man did not come to be served, but to serve..."

-Mark 10:45

Foreword

"Dr. Barrett writes straight from the heart in this inspirational book. His words raise our awareness of the nurturing that our bodies need from us, so that we may enjoy the quality of life that we so often seek through other, more artificial means."

"Through accounts of his own experiences, testimonials from patients and quotes from the Bible, Dr. Barrett inspires us to be mindful of how our bodies are meant to be treated."

"He also gives us a wake up call on how badly we abuse our bodies through prescription drugs, unhealthy diets and the inevitable, unnecessary surgeries that follow."

"Encouraging the reader to adopt a far-reaching level of consciousness about health and healing, Dr. Barrett motivates us to provide a healthy lifestyle for ourselves and our loved ones. He encourages us to bridge the gap between race, social status and religious beliefs so as to take responsibility for each other's health and healing."

"We learn that "alternative" methods of well-being, based on the body's innate ability to heal itself through natural means, is not new. It is centuries old. Its success has been proven time and time again. It is a belief system that must replace the pill popping, symptom—masking one mankind has accepted."

"Dr. Barrett gives us more than good cause to oppose our society's quick-fix mentality. His message empowers us with logical, yet soul stirring reasons to resist the current "norm"—and to pass the word on."

"I hope that Dr. Barrett will follow up with more writings. His conviction is contagious...a healthy addiction by today's standards."

Deborah Da Silva
Freelance Editor

"Whoever saves one
Life saves the
World entire".
(From the movie, "Schindler's List")

Chapter 1

One God, One Light—Sharing The Light

It has been my experience that many (and I might go as far as to say most) people who are entrepreneurs have a strong and abiding faith in God. This seems to be especially true in certain groups of multi-level marketing companies. These people that have a strong desire to be more, to be independent, to be captain of their own ship, usually have God at the helm. After all, it is a scary world out there. Sometimes when you are an entrepreneur, or sole proprietor, whether you are in an M.L.M., or work from your home, it can seem like you are alone in the world and the only one who may be experiencing a particular set of problems or difficulties. You may have the sensation of being like the emperor with his new clothes. This, after all, is not the most wonderful and ingratiating feeling.

In fact, it can be downright scary and nerve racking to make the decision to venture out from under the perceived security veil of a company in which you are just an employee. Individuals who take that first step have great desire, hope, belief and passion in order to take that step into the unknown and great uncertainty. They must have a confidence in themselves, but beyond that, they must have a great belief and faith in a higher power, in God. This is because God is the only one you can trust when times are hard, when you start to doubt yourself, or the economy (economic forecast), or mother nature, or the myriad of other difficulties that can beset the small business man or woman. Many would like to believe that they could trust and rely on friends, family, or a spouse. But ultimately, they can only trust in a higher power, in God and the spirit inside that is of God. After all, where does all this inner strength and desire for a better life, a better world, come from? It has to come from within. It has to come from where God lives, within us!

It is God who is there with us in the good days and the bad days; when all is going right and on those days when things go wrong. It is the faith in God that can carry us through and make us persevere even when we start to waver, become tired and lose faith in ourselves.

It is the story of the man walking along the beach:

Footprints

" One night a man had a dream. He dreamed he was walking along the beach with the Lord. Across the sky flashed scenes from his life. For each scene, he noticed two sets of footprints in the sand; one belonged to him, and the other to the Lord.

When the last scene of his life flashed before him, he looked back at the footprints in the sand. He noticed that many times along the path of his life there was only one set of footprints. He also noticed that it happened at the very lowest and saddest times in his life.

This really bothered him and he questioned the Lord about it. 'Lord, you said that once I decided to follow you, you'd walk with me all the way. But I have noticed that during the most troublesome times in my life, there is only one set of footprints. I don't understand why when I needed you most you would leave me.'

The Lord replied, 'My precious, precious child, I love you and I would never leave you. During your times of trial and suffering, when you see only one set of footprints, it was then that I carried you".
Author unknown

It is the desire to make a better way for our families, for ourselves, and for our fellow man that pushes us onward to pursue and achieve success and greatness. But greatness cannot be achieved without God. God can be many things to many people. People who are spiritual or religious can overcome all odds and adversities. Some believe in Christ, in God the Father, in the Holy Spirit. Others believe in Buddha, Allah, or a universal intelligence. But there is always a higher power than man.

My beliefs are in the Holy Trinity and I know that all that I have accomplished in life is through the grace and goodness of God, the working of Jesus Christ, and the Holy Spirit in my life. I have been to various multi-level marketing meetings, and have seen the intense spirituality of many of the members and the total indomitable spirit, which they display. They will attain their desires by placing total faith and trust in God and their own innate abilities. More than that, they give total thanks to God for that which they have, whether it be meager or grand. Whether a small profit or a million, they are giving thanks to God and derive pleasure and support from quoting the Bible.

Whatever particular universal life force you believe in, prayer to that entity can only reinforce your efforts to be a success.

"For nothing is impossible with God".

-Luke 1:37

I learned a long time ago that the "old sayings" have a lot of merit and wisdom to them. Such as, "You can't be all things to all people" or "You can please some of the people some of the time, but you can't please all of the people all of the time".

I am reminded of the Aesop fable of "The Man, the Boy and the Donkey."

There is wisdom in the ages, if we would but stop and listen!

The Man, the Boy and the Donkey

"A man and his son were once going with their donkey to market. As they were walking along by its side a countryman passed them and said: 'You fools, what is a donkey for but to ride upon?'

So the man put the boy on the donkey and they went on their way. But soon they passed a group of men, one of whom said: 'See that lazy youngster, he lets his father walk while he rides'.

So the man ordered his boy to get off, and got on himself. But they hadn't gone far when they passed two women, one of whom said to the other: 'Shame on that lazy lout to let his poor little son trudge along'.

Well, the man didn't know what to do, but at last he took his boy up before him on the donkey. By this time they had come to the town, and the passers by began to jeer and point at them. The man stopped and asked what they were scoffing at. The men said: 'Aren't you ashamed of yourself for overloading that poor donkey with you and your hulking son?'

The man and the boy got off and tried to think what to do. They thought and they thought, till at last they cut down a pole, tied the donkey's feet to it, and raised the pole and the donkey to their shoulders. They went along amid the laughter of all who met them till they came to Market Bridge, when the donkey, getting one of his feet loose, kicked out and caused the boy to drop his end of the pole. In the struggle, the donkey fell over the bridge, and his forefeet being tied together, he was drowned.

'That will teach you,' said an old man who had followed them: 'Please all, and you will please none".

The point I am attempting to make is that many people will view this book differently. I would truly like it to be a book for all people, all the time. The reality is that this may not happen. Someone at some point may be offended by something I have written, although I hope this is not true.

I have used passages from the Bible to lend support and give credence to what I have written. I am a Christian and use quotes from the scriptures. I have also used quotes and passages from other authors. My wishes are that anyone can pick up this book, read the words, and the quotes whether they are Christians, Jews, Buddhists, Christian Scientists, or other and look at them as words of wisdom and truth. This is not a Christian book for Christians only. It is a book for all people interested in health and healing.

"When God gives light he gives it for all".

-Spanish Proverb

There has to be an awareness shift. One must truly realize that we can do nothing alone, that no man is an island. We must see the greater good for humanity. The truth is no man can prosper and survive alone. If He could, God may have stopped with Adam. No, the fact is that life is about unions, companionship, relationships, covenants, marriage, friendships, and togetherness. "Two are better than one..."

"...if one falls down, his friend can help him up".

-Ecclesiastes 4:9-10

Even prisoners who have so much rage and hate inside them, if put in solitary confinement for too long will go insane. Human beings need other human beings. And it is each of our responsibility to care for one another. Spreading or disseminating truthful information on health and healing products can save the world. I have seen many people involved in multi-level marketing. I am convinced that most have a deeply rooted and powerful spiritual belief and guidance. Even if money was a primary motivator for getting involved with a company, I believe that these people believe in their product and know they can make a difference in another life. Making money for money's sake is not worthwhile. There must be a higher purpose for life, a higher purpose to sell those herbs, vitamins and minerals. People do know this. People know it innately, even if they have not acknowledged it yet on a conscious level. It is the people involved in M.L.M. that will do more good for more people by selling nutritional products. These individuals who join M.L.M. display a strong sense of purpose, drive, will and determination. They are highly motivated to succeed. And from what I have seen, they have a strong and deep religious belief in God. They are in touch with the spiritual side of their being. These qualities (components) coupled with high quality nutritional products can change the world. It can change the face of human beings from that of weakness, illness or despair, to that of health, vibrancy and vitality. These people and all the others who promote herbs can elevate and change the health of the planet.

"You are the light of the world...Let your light so shine before men, that they may see your good works and glorify your Father in heaven".

-Matthew 5:13

Is it dark? If so, do not despair,

for the sun will yet rise.

...And when the morning comes,

light, warmth, joy, and healing

are soon to follow after."

- Charles H. Spurgeon

Chapter 2

Healed by Morning

Nightingale Conant Corporation is a name that many of you know. They produce motivational audiocassettes from great people, leaders in the field, highly successful people like Joe Vitale, Napolean Hill, Anthony Robbins, Zig Zigler and many more.

A letter I received from Vic Conant contained a quote from Mark Twain. It read:

"Inherently, each one of us has the substance within to achieve whatever our goals and dreams define. What is missing from each of us is the training, education and insight to utilize what we already have".

Isn't that incredibly powerful? There is such truth and strength in that statement. Some of you want to heal yourselves, some want to heal others, some want to change the face of the planet by changing the health and face of humanity. Others want to profit from the 4.5 billion-dollar business of the herbal market. Whatever your motivation is, I believe that you will find some power and wisdom in this book. I hope that I will provide you with some knowledge, education, and insight that will inspire you to achieve your goals and dreams. And in turn, enrich and empower the lives of others to achieve their goals and dreams.

"The people who make a difference are not the ones with the credentials, but the ones with the concern".

-Max Lucado

The title of this book is meant to be thought provoking not necessarily a reality. It is not meant to suggest, imply or guarantee that by reading this book you will be healed by morning. However, it is something that we all want when we are ill, isn't it? In fact, we would rather be healed now, on the spot, because we do not have time to be sick. Have you ever heard, said, or thought those words? Of course you have, we all have.

Well, the title came into existence through a conversation I had with a wonderful friend of mine, Joe Vitale. We were having lunch, discussing some of his latest adventures and just catching up. You see Joe is a great author of many books and had just returned from a trip to Chicago where he was taping a new audiocassette program for Nightengale Conant. As he was recounting his story to me, he told me that he had not felt well before he went on the trip. By the time he returned home, he was very sick due to many factors. As I am also Joe's chiropractor, I, of course, listened intently.

As we talked, Joe said that he was tired of being sick and *did not have time for it*! As he sat at home feeling pretty lousy, he said something very profound to himself … he wanted to be Healed by Morning. It was at this moment, he realized this was a great title for a book.

In fact, Joe and I had been talking about the writing of

this very book for some time but it had remained rough and titleless. As we sat and discussed all the possible meanings of Healed by Morning, it became clearer that this was a perfect title.

In fact, who doesn't want to be Healed by Morning when they are ill? "Just let me be well so I can go on my trip tomorrow," "...just let me be well to go to work," "... let me feel better by the morning". All these statements either go out as some nebulous cry to the universe, are said to a family member, whirl around in our heads never verbalized, or are voiced to God in a prayer.

"Please, God, let me be well by morning".

Somehow, the morning is always the dawn of a new beginning. It is the point at which new and better things begin. It is when all the bad from the day or the night before is to be washed away, a fresh start. It is a grand and magical time when the clean, fresh light of the new day cleanses all that was wrong, ill, or bad with the world. As though the simple process of sleep will start the healing process of the mind, body or soul and all will be okay.

We have all heard statements like... "Just sleep on it and everything will be better in the morning". In truth, much healing does take place as the body rests. The body needs time to heal and recuperate through sleep. It is a time of rebuilding and regenerating. Joe's words, "Healed by Morning", were so wonderfully profound because they conjure up many different thoughts. Is it realistic to believe we can actually be Healed by Morning? Or is this just something we want because we live in such an impatient and hurried world with everything instant, pop up, quick fix, done in under 60 seconds?

I personally believe many things can be Healed by Morning depending upon how much effort we put into it and how much faith we have in it actually happening.

"Now faith is being sure of what we hope for and certain of what we do not see".

-Hebrews 11:1

Of course, there is the other question of which morning will we be healed by. All things are possible with God if we truly have faith and trust. But, how many of us actually do? I am talking about the absolute certainty, not a moments doubt or hesitation kind of faith. The kind of faith Indiana Jones displayed in the movie, "The Last Crusade". Indiana Jones was searching for the Holy Grail, the chalice Christ used at the Last Supper. As he had outsmarted every trap laid for him, he came to a chasm with no apparent way across. At this point, no amount of logical thinking or intelligence could handle the obstacle before him. He remembered the words, which had earlier been told to him. He must have a leap in faith.

At this point, all that was left was to have an unshakable faith in God, and trust that He would carry him through to success. Indiana Jones took one big step in faith, literately stepping out over the edge into what appeared to be a bottomless chasm. As he did so, he landed on a natural stone bridge that could not be seen from his previous position. We may not always be able to see.

The things that are true and real may not yet be visible to us. Our problems, life or bad health may seem like a bottomless chasm. But if we walk in faith, God will provide all our needs to be met! We must believe!

If our faith and belief were so unwaving, so unshakably strong that we could be healed, or that we could not even get sick, then I do not believe any disease or sickness could ever touch us or have power over us. We would be immune or impenetrable from foreign invaders. We would achieve a higher state of existence. We would achieve ultimate health and wellness.

Unfortunately, most of us do not have this higher order of thinking, this ultimate state of consciousness. So we are left to proclaim a statement or prayer to be healed. Or merely express a hope or wish without any real substance behind it. Like we would hope to win the lottery. But again, can't we or shouldn't we be able to be healed rapidly?

I believe that if our faith was so strong and without any Achilles heel, that it could not be shattered, we could heal rapidly. A faith so strong, that when prayer is put out to God for healing, we could expect to be healed. But our faith and focus has to be tremendously strong and intact. There is no room for even a moment's worth of doubt because that will cause the whole thing to crumble. Sickness feeds on doubt. After all, we read about it time and again in the Bible. Stories of faith and doubt and their consequences.

Remember what happened to Peter in the story of Jesus walking on the water? Peter wanted to join Jesus on the water. "He got down out of the boat, walked on the water and came toward Jesus. But when he saw the wind, he was afraid and beginning to sink, cried out, 'Lord, save me'! Immediately, Jesus reached out His hand and caught him. 'You of little faith,' He said, 'Why did you doubt?'" Peter could have actually walked on that water and been safe through Jesus' power and love, had he strong enough faith, faith in Jesus and faith in his own innate ability.

So too can it be for us, that if we send up a prayer to God, we need to have faith that He will come to our aid. Maybe this aid will not be as direct as we would like it. Perhaps we will be sent to travel down a certain road for healing or asked to participate in our own healing through the use of herbs or other means. Maybe the healing will come in God's time and not ours.

Maybe God is just waiting for our faith to be so incredibly strong that it is almost automatic like our lungs taking a breath of air. We do not think about, question or doubt it. It just happens! As a pure instinctual reflex! Perhaps, the healing will come by morning, but maybe not tomorrow morning. Perhaps, the one after, or the one after that.

So this book, "Healed by Morning", can be many things to many readers. But, hopefully, with quotes from scripture and positive affirmations, logic, facts and truth, it will lead you down a road of natural healing, and bring about an awareness of what God wants of you and your responsibility toward your own healing and the healing of others.

"For wisdom will enter your heart, and knowledge will be pleasant to your soul. Discretion will protect you, and understanding will guard you".

-Proverbs 2:10-11

As Creator, God knows more about our bodies, His creation than we could ever discover either through philosophy or science."

-Reginald Cherry

Chapter 3

Responsibility - A Freedom Of Choice Granted By God

One Sunday as I sat in church and listened to the priest's sermon, he spoke about the beggar who had been blind from birth. The passage is as follows:

"As he went along, he saw a man blind from birth..." "...he spit on the ground, made some mud with the saliva, and put it on the man's eyes. 'Go', he told him, 'wash in the Pool of Siloam' (this word means sent). So the man went and washed, and came home seeing".

-John 9: 1-7

The Pharisees did not want to believe that this man was healed so simply. Just as many in traditional allopathic medicine want to turn their backs to the healing that can be accomplished through natural means. Whether that be through prayer, spiritual healing, or natural therapies, such as herbs and nutritional supplements, or chiropractic and acupuncture.

The priest's words struck me as quite profound. He said Jesus allowed this man to cooperate in his own healing by telling him to go to the Pool of Siloam and wash his eyes. Jesus could certainly have healed this man with a word, a touch, or wave of the hand, but what He actually did was to have him join in and take some responsibility for his own healing. God gave us free will and the ability to make choices. Jesus gave this beggar an opportunity to make a choice.

The beggar could have stayed right where he was and not attempted to go to the waters, or he could have rebelled and given many excuses why he did not want to go or why he did not think he should. He could have professed that he had too many obstacles to overcome. He could have questioned the purpose in trying, or he could have procrastinated. But he made the immediate decision to follow Jesus' request and the results were miraculous!

God still allows us free will. We still can make choices and centuries later, God is still capable of curing all. But He does ask us to participate in our own healing and He leaves it up to us to decide on the type of healing that we partake in. God knows what is best for us. He knows what will heal us the quickest, but He allows us to choose. We can choose to destroy our lives and run our bodies into the ground or we can choose to live a good life. Healing and health does not and should not just begin when we notice the first signs or symptoms of sickness. It should begin with proper prevention of ill health.

This is becoming increasingly difficult in today's toxic world. However, it can be done with proper spirituality, vitamins, herbs, diet, exercise, chiropractic and refraining from haphazardly dumping toxins into our bodies such as over-the-counter drugs, prescription drugs, alcohol, tobacco, fast food and other substances of little or no nutritional value.

Are you aware of the most recent study that identified

more than 106,000 people die each year from properly prescribed medication? And that over two million more become seriously ill? This could possibly make drug side effects the fourth most common cause of death in the United States!

Drugs and improper living are killing us! I know this sounds harsh, but sometimes reality is harsh. Is there a possible solution? Yes. God wants us to be healthy and stay away from drugs.

"Beloved, I wish above all things that thou mayest prosper and be in good health".

-III John 2

He has given us His plants and now we know how to use them. Then God said:

"I give you every seed bearing plant on the face of the whole earth and every tree that has fruit with seed in it. They will be yours for food".

-Genesis 1:29

If they are ours for food, then this should be all we need to sustain us and give us health. This food is designed to not only nourish us, but also provide for our health and healing. God provided for us through natural means so that everything we need is within our grasp. God expects us to be healthy and use natural means to maintain our health.

A person who is not totally committed to themselves truly getting well will make excuses why they can not get well such as, they have no time, or it's too expensive. They may claim that they can not sell herbs or buy herbs to heal or why they should use drugs and not natural remedies. What they project they shall expect. In other words, if they believe they have so much in life to keep them from getting well, that is exactly what will happen. They will never get well!

"God gives every bird its food but does not thrust it into its nest".

-Danish Proverb

However, if a true belief of healing is present, and one utilizes internal intelligence, faith, and prayer, and then listens for the answers and pathways to healing, miracles will follow.

You may be familiar with Napolean Hill, a mastermind for success. He is responsible for elevating the financial health of millions of people. He also spoke and wrote about our spirit or life force, universal intelligence—God. I have transcribed one of his audiotapes for you because it speaks to the healing of a human being and the faith and trust in God one must have in order for healing to occur. He speaks about applied faith.

Allowing your mind to be open to the inflow of power from infinite intelligence which will guide you to achieve the desired result that you want. This is applied faith and it works in the healing of the mind and body.

Napolean recounts a story about his son, who at the time of his birth was born without ears. The two doctors who delivered the boy were actually the newborn's uncles. They told Napolean Hill that other babies had been born this way (without ears) and none of them were ever able to hear at all and did not learn to speak. Apparently, they were attempting to prepare Mr. Hill for the inevitable reality that his new son would be a deaf mute. Well, Mr. Hill stopped the doctors and told them that even though he had not even seen his son yet that his son would in fact "go through life with 100 percent of his hearing just like normal children".

One of the doctors continued telling him some things in life can not be changed so he might as well accept it. Hill refused and told them that "there isn't anything in this world that I can't do something about. If it's nothing more than adjust myself to an unpleasant circumstance so that it doesn't break my heart I can do that." Napolean says, "I started immediately to do just that. I made up my mind before I saw my son that under no circumstances was I going to accept him as a deaf mute. Under no circumstances was I going to accept his condition as an affliction, under no circumstances was I going to stop until he had 100 percent of his hearing. I had no idea how it was going to come about, the only thing that I was sure about is, that it was going to come about and I want to tell you that when you go at anything with that attitude you are using applied faith."

"I went to work on my child before I even saw him with prayer and for the next four years I spent at least four hours a day working on him communicating with him through his subconscious mind, and up to the eighteenth month we knew positively that nothing happened. But that didn't destroy my faith. I knew something would happen. We kept on working on him. We gave him every test available as to his hearing and he wasn't hearing anything up to eighteen months. And then a strange thing happened. We knew that he was hearing, but we didn't know how much.

I could snap my fingers while standing behind him and he would turn to see which way the noise was coming from and we knew that he was hearing. By the time he was four years of age he had developed 65 percent of his normal hearing through my prayers and communications through his subconscious mind. Which of the two did the most good I don't know. Maybe it was the combination of the two. By the end of the fourth year we had developed enough of his normal hearing to get him through the graded school, high school and the third year in college.

And during the third year in college, the Acoustics Company who makes hearing aids, heard about this unusual case. It was the only one of its kind in the world, where a child born without ears had learned to hear and speak. They came down to the University of West Virginia at Morgan Town and made my son a special hearing aid that gave him the other 35 percent of his normal hearing. And today he has 100 percent of his normal hearing just like I said he would have".

"Doctors came from all over the world. They made hundreds and hundreds of x-rays of his brain after they found out that 65 percent of his normal hearing had been developed. They wanted to find out if they could find any physical organs through which he was hearing, and they never found any. They never did. And another queer thing about it, Blair could hear just as well with his hearing aid on his spine as he can with it on his head.

It was a great blessing because it enabled me to learn about the power of prayer as I would never have learned from any other source... I threw my heart and soul into this child and I made up my mind that if there was any cause, if there was any God I was going to get through to Him and I was going to get a response. And I got through and I got the response! There is no such thing as impossibility that prayers can do anything and everything!

Believe and it will happen!

"I tell you the truth, if anyone says to this mountain, 'Go, throw yourself into the sea', and does not doubt in his heart but believes that what he says will happen, it will be done for him. Therefore, I tell you, whatever you ask for in prayer, believe that you have received it, and it will be yours".

-Mark 11:23

He Touches

He touches lives
He touches hearts
He touches us, to not live apart.

He touches minds
He touches souls
He touches us, to make us whole.

He touches sickness
He touches health
He touches us, to become His wealth.

He touches feelings
He touches hurts
He touches us, not just in Heaven,
but here on Earth.

He touches you
He touches me
He touches to, fulfill God's destiny.

-Patty Hoelker

Chapter 4

W. W. J. D.?

You see these letters on wristbands, T-shirts, ball caps, jewelry and more. They represent the words, What Would Jesus Do? Perhaps you have seen these words. But, of course, they are more than mere words, they represent a thought, a concept, a way of acting and doing, a lifestyle. It is something that should be thought of during every moment of one's existence. It is a template for correctness, for moral and righteous behavior.

It means to have a person stop and think (the operable word) about what they are to do, say and even think before they do it and look at it through another's eyes. Yes, look through Jesus' eyes, if upon reflection one can say Jesus would not do that, then perhaps it is not morally correct and therefore should not be done. It is a way of self monitoring and hopefully encouraging one and shaping one into a more loving, forgiving and Godly individual. To try and walk the walk, and talk the talk, and aspire to be more like Jesus, to walk in His footsteps (if that is even humanly possible).

"Your ears will hear a voice behind you, saying, 'This is the way, walk in it'".

-Isaiah 30:21

This makes me stop and truly ponder that question from a totally different point of view.

If Jesus were here today, if He were actually born into

today's world, (befitting to ponder at this new millennium) what would He do, what would He think about today's health care? How would He feel about the cloning of humans, surrogate mothers, or fertility clinics?

What would Jesus do? What would He do about the rampant over utilization of prescription and non prescription drugs, and the countless unnecessary surgeries, the total disregard for the human structure, the careless removal of body parts, and the subdued nature of our innate intelligence to express itself?

I know that Jesus would support natural healing since in fact, He was the ultimate natural healer! What is being dubbed today as "alternative medicine" is really true natural healing the way it should be. It is what should be considered mainstream. Allopathic medicine—(that of drugs and surgery) should actually be considered alternative medicine and utilized as a back up or secondary system when natural healing is not enough or needs some support.

I am certain that Jesus would be opposed to those things that were harmful or toxic to the human body.

Can you imagine Jesus walking around on Prozac or endorsing children being subjected to a Class II controlled substance called Ritalin? I do not believe He would be supportive of the drugging of the world through the use of prescription or non-prescription drugs. Of pumping our livestock with drugs to make them plumper, which eventually affects the humans that eat them. In fact, He would condemn these things!

I do believe He would be in favor of natural healing methods that would allow the innate intelligence of the body to function at its optimum state and He would support those who work with the physical body for the greater good of the body. Thus, we would have the ability to actually be Healed by Morning. I believe Jesus would be in favor of chiropractic, acupuncture, massage, Qigong, vitamin therapy, herbs, magnets, essential oils and many other forms of natural healing, everything and anything that is true and non-invasive to the body. Do you believe it is possible to drug the body to the point where the drugs actually suppress innate and interfere with its ability to be freely expressed?

It is now becoming harder to create a positive life changing healing experience in humans that are walking around with drugs in their bodies. One example of this is how drugs dampen, squelch, interfere, and impede with the ability of the brain and the nervous system to work properly.

Without becoming complex, let's just take a brief look at neuroanatomy. Certain chemical substances are known to be transmitters of nerve information. There are over thirty of these substances and they are called neurotransmitters. Some are amines like dopamine and serotonin. Others may be amino acids like glycine and glutamate, and still others may be peptides such as endorphins and insulin. They are all highly important and critical to proper brain and nervous system function.

A simplistic example of how the nervous system works is much like putting a key into a lock. The lock will only accept the key that is designed to fit it properly. The proper fit allows a sequence of action to take place thereby locking or unlocking the mechanism. However, if a similar key was put into the lock and broken off, it would now occupy that space. Attempting to put a second key (the correct key) into the lock would be futile. Therefore, no further action could be initiated.

Drugs work in a similar fashion; they interfere with the ability of these neurotransmitters to function properly. One chemical transmitter, serotonin, is known to have an effect on our sense of well being, happiness, appetites, and sex drive. Too little serotonin may cause depression while too much may cause a person to be overly enthusiastic. The drug, Prozac, is used to control the transmission of serotonin.

The body is a highly complex organism. Although, we have great knowledge of it, much of the details of how it works still need to be learned. Foreign chemicals introduced into the body will have an effect. Some of these effects are known, but not fully. When more than one drug is introduced, then there can be no predictability. When a drug is introduced, it sets off a chain of events to the extent of undetermined repercussions. Our actions can be far reaching beyond what we can hypothesize. Much like a chain of dominoes that once the first is knocked down, it is hard to stop, and the dominoes can take many routes, some of which we can't see the end result.

Prozac has never been approved for anyone under 18 years of age, yet it is routinely prescribed. There are over 1.5 million children on anti-depressants in the United States. Can we really know the extent of the damage that these drugs are extolling on these yet developing young individuals? No, we can't!

In fact, mounting suspicion and evidence is pointing to many of our current problems in society. Suicides and shootings are directly linked to psychotropic drugs. Even many medical doctors are speaking out against the use of these drugs. The evidence definitely points to many of our school shootings as a result of suicidal and violent behavior caused by psychotropic drugs. The research and the data is available. It only takes a reasonable and open-minded individual to look at it and realize the truth and the enormity of the problem at hand if a change is not made. The drugging of our children and us with mind-altering substances is not a reasonable or acceptable pathway to health and healing.

So, what would Jesus do? Well — what did Jesus do? "Jesus as the great physician focused much of His early ministry on two activities—healing and teaching".* Why not become more like Jesus? How better to follow in His footsteps than to help heal the planet through natural means, by educating the masses as to the potential for healing naturally and to the devastating dangers of drugs!

*Reginald Cherry

Think about it! Would Jesus want His brothers and sisters to be subjected to the side effects of drugs, such a as suicide and depression? Children hold a special place in the eyes and heart of God.

We have to ask ourselves, what are we doing to our children and our future? All of this because we are too lazy, too tired, or use the excuses of not having the time, the energy or the money to seek alternatives, or spend time with our kids. People tend to follow the path of least resistance. The pharmaceutical companies seem to know this. It is much easier to pick up a pill, swallow it, and believe all your problems have been solved. However, this is not reality. Our problems have only yet to begin!

YOUR CHILD MAY BE DEPRESSED AND SUICIDAL BECAUSE OF THEIR ACNE DRUG

The FDA warned doctors and consumers about the side effects of the drug, Accutane in February of 1998. Accutane is used to cure acne but can cause "depression, psychosis and rarely suicidal thoughts and actions". The FDA admitted to receiving reports of severe psychological side effects for more than 10 years. Is acne worth losing your child over?

W. W. J. D.?

From "Important New Safety Information about Accutane", Food and Drug Administration, February 25, 1998, Health Watch, Volume 2, Number 12

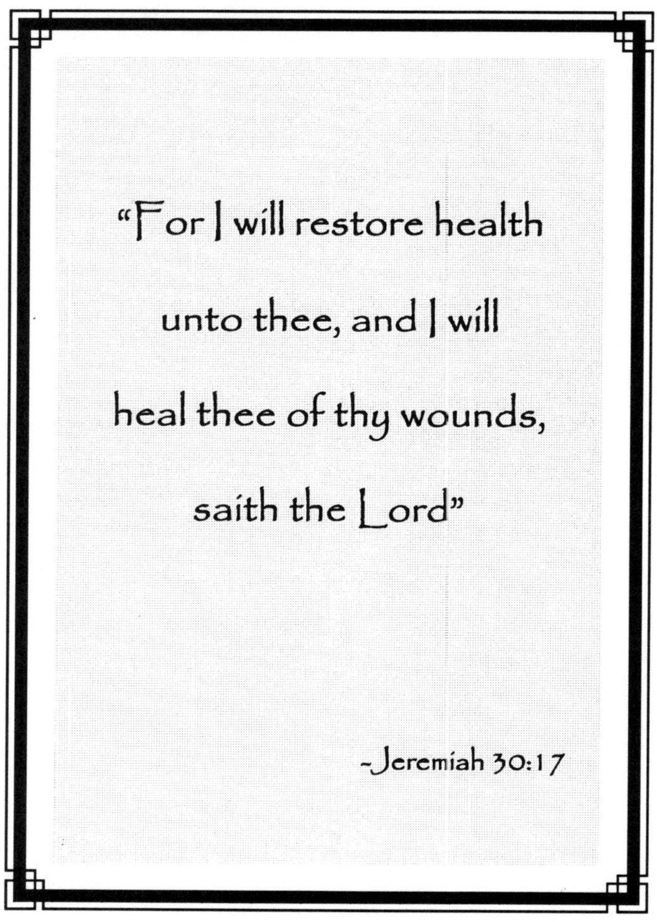

"For I will restore health unto thee, and I will heal thee of thy wounds, saith the Lord"

-Jeremiah 30:17

Chapter 5

The Search For Healing And Longevity

What do we want from life? The list may include cars, planes, boats, vacations, jewelry, money, home, swimming pools, time with our families, good health, travel, and material goods of all kinds. When all these things are distilled down into the one basic thing we want—it is right in front of us—we want life, we want to live, to survive and to enjoy our survival! We want the fountain of youth. This seems especially true of the current generation of baby boomers that are reaching new plateaus. They are growing older and have the money to attempt putting the brakes on aging.

These aging baby boomers are finding that they ache a little bit more when they work out or play sports. They can not burn the candle at both ends the way they used to when they were younger. Perhaps, they are feeling a little stiff and they are slow to move in the mornings. They can't just pop out of bed and go anymore. Those foods that they inhaled as kids are now becoming a problem for their digestive systems.

Now, reading glasses seem to be part of their daily routine. Their hair is turning gray or disappearing. Gravity is taking its toll and body parts are beginning to sag and exhibit the weight of time. Muscles that were once taken for granted are less toned, and it is harder to tone them anyway. A few extra calories or grams of fat seem to stack the weight on in pounds and always in the wrong places. The younger generations seem to be more annoying and where do they get their energy? So after all is said and done, and the toys lose their interest...What is everyone looking for? Life! But not just life—a healthy, vibrant, young again life. Who wouldn't mind living to 150 years old, if it felt like 30 or 40?

"Every man desires to live long; yet no man desires to be old".

-Jonathen Swift

So people are looking for anti-aging and disease prevention. The U.S. Census Bureau reports that 10,000 people turn 50 every day. Unfortunately, it seems that society is actually becoming sicker.

It is not uncommon for people who are 30, 40 or 50 to actually say they feel like 80, 90 or over 100! A question I routinely ask patients is, "How old do you feel?" I have had some patients in their 20's actually say they feel over 100 years of age! This is a problem. It lets me know that their health has been neglected and the overall health of this country is on the decline. Why?

It is a question of balance. Human beings are pushing themselves harder than they ever have in the history of the world with little or no regard to the consequences of their actions. Proper prevention of sickness and disease is practiced by very few. Maintenance of the structure is all but forgotten.

Proper fueling of the body is extremely difficult in today's age and usually not even cared about. The term for the late nineties has been "extreme". Everything in excess, abundance, full out, no fear! This encompasses the entirety of many lives, not just in sports. Yet in sports, we are demanding our bodies to do more and usually without proper support and conditioning. We want to run faster, jump higher, carry more, and lift more.

How long can a human body survive on inadequate sleep, too many activities, trauma, fast food, high fat, high sugar, and chemicals both in the food (food additives) and out, like smoking, alcohol, recreational drugs and medical drugs?

We must attempt to restore balance to the body in order to achieve health. The following diagram should give you the idea.

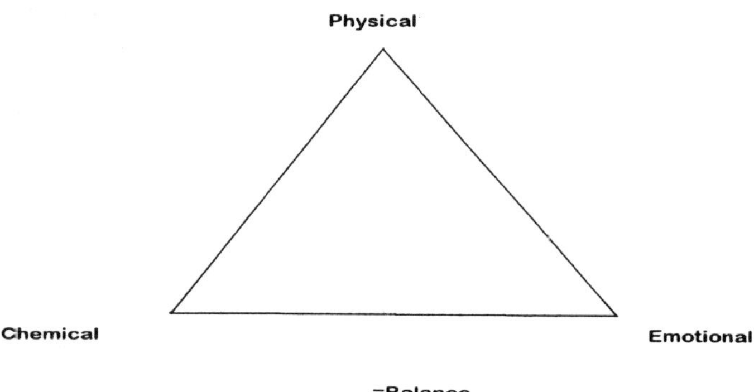

Balance between these 3 elements = Health

The inter-relationship of this triangle is highly important. One cannot exist without the other. All three are important and affect each other and the whole. When one element of the triangle is affected (suffers) so too does it impact the others. The over all effect is the weakening of the triangle and ultimate destruction. Inevitably, this means that ill health, disease and ultimate death is realized in the human being.

Imbalance in the physical, chemical and emotional aspects of our being can be created by any of the following:

Physical	**Chemical**	**Emotional**
subluxations	physiologic imbalances	financial
(misaligned vertebrae	nutrition	marital
impairing proper nervous	food allergies	academic
system function)	chemical allergies	friends
postural and	environmental sensitivities	peers
biomechanical imbalances	toxic reactions	relationships
trauma	depleted minerals/vitamins	job
		death

One of the questions that I ask during the consultation of every patient, after taking a complete history is, "On a scale of 1 to 10, 10 being the highest, how do you rate your personal commitment to getting well and correcting the cause of your health problems?". I am often surprised at a patient's lack of commitment to themselves and their own health.

They may have just told me that they've had excruciating headaches since childhood, or have only one bowel movement a week, or they have so much pain they don't enjoy their life or family. Yet they may rate themselves a 5, 6, 7, or 8 on the scale. Of course, the question I ask is, "Why?" It is mind boggling how many people answer because of the money. In other words, they value money more than their health.

More money will then be wasted on the pursuit of symptom relief that doesn't solve the problem, until one day their bodies are so overloaded with the problem that other systems fail and eventually the person is debilitated with a physical or mental shut down or both. The problem that may have been solved for hundreds of dollars now costs them thousands. And perhaps they lose family time and work. There is always more to lose by ignoring a problem than handling it as early as possible.

Without the intention to get well and perhaps the momentary sacrifice of some time and money, it is virtually futile to treat a patient who is less committed to getting well, than the doctor's commitment to getting them well.

If an individual is not focused on their purpose to receive help and help themselves to get well, then nothing any one can do will be satisfactory. We have all heard the stories of miracles occurring where science and medicine has written a patient off, but through prayer, inner fortitude, willingness, or intention, these people have baffled science and recovered. That matter of intention and an individual's willingness to survive can not be understated. Adversely, you will find many stories of people who should have healed or lived but their health steadily declined, or they died when they should have responded, thus, baffling doctors again.

Therefore, it is in the power of the spirit, the mind, the innate ability of the body that strength and healing come from.

Whether you are undergoing chiropractic treatment, acupuncture, or treating yourself naturally with herbs and vitamin/mineral therapy, you must make the decision with your heart, body, and soul to get well or no amount of outside intervention will help. You and your wishes will prevail. Your mind and spirit are incredibly powerful. Use it the right way!

Even Jesus poised the question of whether or not an individual wanted to truly heal.

"When Jesus saw him lying there; and knew that he already had been in that condition a long time, he said to him, 'Do you want to be made well?'"

-John 5:6

Well, do you?

"The doctor of the future
will give no medicine
but will interest his patients
in the care of the human
frame,
in diet and in the
cause and prevention
of disease."

-Thomas Edison

Chapter 6

Certainty

"When they came to the crowd, a man approached Jesus and knelt before him. 'Lord have mercy on my son', he said. 'He has seizures and is suffering greatly...' Jesus rebuked the demon, and it came out of the boy, and he was healed from that moment. Then the disciples came to Jesus in private and asked, 'Why couldn't we drive it out?' He replied, 'Because you have so little faith. I tell you the truth if you have faith as small as a mustard seed you can say to this mountain, move from here to there, and it will move. Nothing will be impossible for you'".

-Matthew 17:14-21

Over the next several pages, you will see targets, which display different levels of certainty. The target represents what a person might believe his faith and absolute certainty is in a product, service, or idea. It also represents where others might fall in their belief of the same thing. These targets will take you through absolute certainty in natural healing as shown by the following target all the way through to non-certainty or aberrant thinking.

ABSOLUTE CERTAINTY

(Natural Healing)

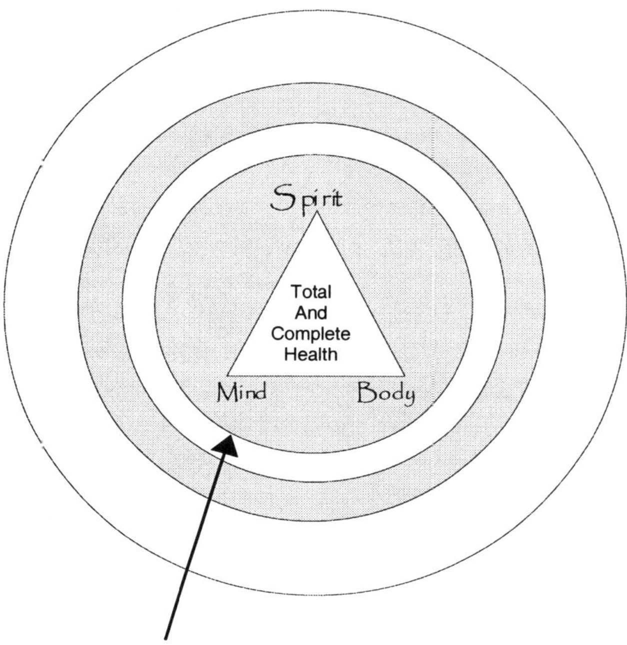

To achieve this, your belief system must be unquestionably strong and be in the center of the target.

-The power that made the body can heal the body.

-The body can heal when innate intelligence is released from the outside influences that inhibit it. Allowing the nervous system to properly control and regulate the body.

Herbs/Essential Oils/Vitamins/Minerals/Chiropractic/Natural Healing Methods

WHERE DOES YOUR CERTAINTY FALL?

WHERE IS YOUR CERTAINTY?

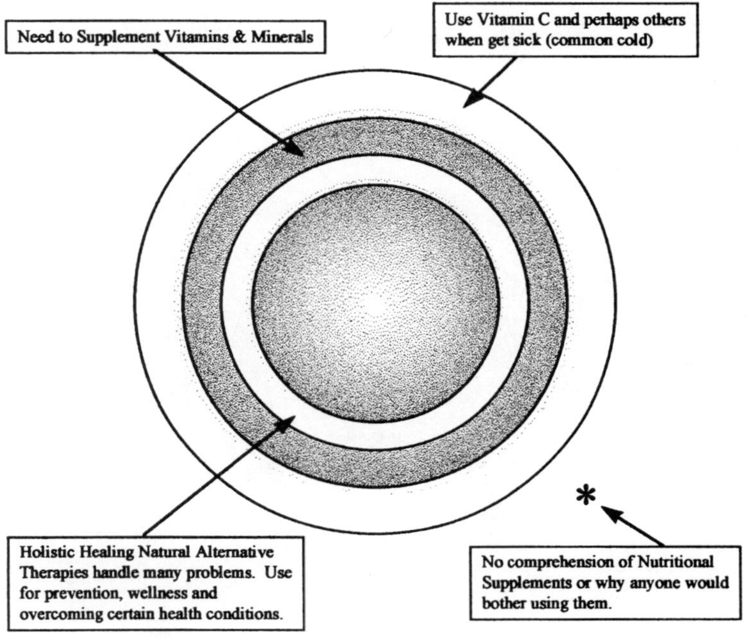

An example of non-certainty of natural healing or aberrant thinking has been displayed for years by much of the medical profession. Many medical doctors have been trying to invalidate the use of herbs and vitamins/minerals as well as any alternative health treatment. What they consider to be non-conventional and unscientific. In fact, many still do. Some have even said it is a waste of money to take herbs or vitamins, but take them if you want expensive urine. These people are nowhere near the center of the target. They are ignorant to or lack knowledge of the subject. They may even be off the target completely.

ABERRANT THINKING
(WHAT MANY ERRONEOUSLY BELIEVE!)

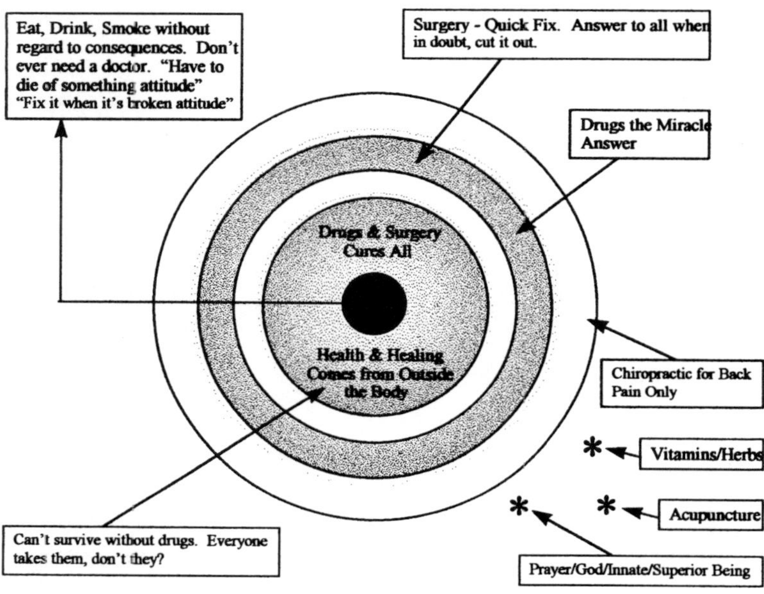

The average person is learning more and the statistics show it. Forty-six percent of surveyed people in 1997, said they have used alternative medicine practitioners. The population is now seeking alternative medicine such as chiropractic, herbs, and acupuncture. Harvard researchers found that Americans have made 629 million visits to alternative medicine practitioners compared with 386 million visits to primary care doctors! They are taking responsibility for their health and are empowering themselves with knowledge of natural health methods. These people may be somewhat closer to the center of the target and to the reality of the quality and quantity of health that can be achieved through these means.

But remember most people haven't reached this level of awareness and in fact, many of you reading this book haven't, either. But as you read more and increase your base of knowledge or you use and sell nutritional products you will see miracles happen. You will be witness to powerful healing, that many will not understand and others will try to minimize or explain away. You will hear incredible testimonies from friends, relatives, and others that have used the herbs. Perhaps, even herbs you have suggested, and as this occurs, your certainty of health and healing of herbs will increase.

You will, in fact, become more confident, more aware, and you will be moving closer and closer to the center of the target where you will know that all things are possible. You will realize that total health can be achieved and that herbs, vitamins/minerals are essential to the healthy existence of the physical, human form and that we are in control of our health. God has provided everything we need for our ultimate healthy survival on this planet in a natural form.

"Fruit trees of all kinds will grow on both banks of the river...Their fruit will serve for food and their leaves for healing".

-Ezekiel 47:12

You will see that awareness comes in the center of the target and realize that health actually comes from above, down, inside and out. You will also realize that you are an incredible vibrant being that has an innate intelligence with the ability to heal and actually be superior to disease and outside influences.

Og Mandino in relaying God's instructions to mankind writes,

"You are capable of great wonders. Your potential is unlimited... You are the greatest miracle in the world".

Therefore, you must be superior to sickness and disease!

In order to heal then, our faith in a higher power to heal us and our faith in our own ability of self-healing has to be unquestionably strong! Beyond that, we must not allow any of our innate abilities to be interfered with or diminished by extraneous forces that dampen, weaken, or impinge upon it. Drugs then, of any sort, only serve to undermine the free expression of the universal powers to perform. Seemingly, all use of non-destructive means of therapy to enhance or magnify our body's inner abilities and our ability to invoke spiritual aid must be utilized.

For example, prayer can be very powerful all alone, but miracles have been witnessed and attested to when people ask for help from others, such as praying to the Saints, forming a prayer group, prayer lines, healing masses or services. Collective imagery, visualization or prayer only serves to establish a pure and focused concentration for positive result. Much like a magnifying glass can harness and focus the amazing power of the sun. When used properly, that power can be used to create a conflagration. Using treatments and therapies that enhance the body's innate or electrical and magnetic properties, such as chiropractic, acupuncture, healing touch, massage, magnetic therapy, herbs, vitamins/minerals, megatherapy, or Qigong can have a synergistic effect. We must attempt to restore balance to the body in order to achieve health.

As a chiropractor, I have seen and heard some amazing stories of healing which are powerful testimonies to the human spirit. My belief in innate intelligence in the power of the body is dead center in the target. For example, I know that chiropractic has been and is instrumental in helping people with allergies, sinuses, ear infections, digestive disturbances, ringing in the ears, visual disturbances, headaches, fatigue, irritability, and more. But do you realize the average person has no concept of this? It creates total confusion in their mind. If you were to say, go to a chiropractor for those ear infections or take your child, the person might think you were crazy or stupid. Even many of those who think they know chiropractic but have never been, just believe chiropractors help with back problems, neck problems and perhaps headaches.

They are way on the outer ring of the target. The outer ring of understanding the depth and breadth of what chiropractic can do to enhance their lives and their health. But still only 7 to 10 percent of the population sees a chiropractor, because most people do not even begin to comprehend chiropractic's benefits. In fact, they are not even hitting the target at all. They are unaware that chiropractors work with a person's nervous system to remove any interference that might be weakening it and negatively impacting an individual's health.

The common man, although highly intelligent, hasn't been educated to truly understand that the nervous system controls and regulates virtually every cell, tissue, chemical, enzyme, and organs of their bodies. If they did, 100 percent of the population would see a chiropractor before they ever went to their medical doctor. They would routinely have this vitally important nervous system checked and analyzed for proper function. And they would have periodic body "tune ups" to ensure optimum function and capability to reach and maintain peak performance. That is why I wrote my first book, **"Dare to Break Through the Pain-** ***A Guide to Eliminating Back & Neck Pain Naturally Without Drugs or Surgery!"***

I believe everyone on the planet needs and deserves chiropractic care to enhance their life, not just when they are in pain. I am a bull's eye on the absolute certainty natural healing target—dead center! Which target are you on? Use the targets on the following pages to evaluate your belief system, take a red pen and plug in the numbers. Then by the end of the book, you can re-evaluate yourself and see if you have moved to a different target or closer to the center. My hope is that you gain enough insight and understanding to move to the center of the certainty target. My prayer is that you are motivated to cooperate with God to bring optimal health to your life and to the lives of your loved ones.

Absolute Certainty

1. The power that made the body can heal the body.

2. The body can heal when innate intelligence is released from the outside influences that inhibit it. Allowing the nervous system to properly control and regulate the body. (Chiropractic healing)

3. Natural holistic healing methods (chiropractic, herbs/vitamins/ minerals)

4. Acupuncture/magnetic therapies/etc.

5. Prayer/God/Superior Being

6. Use natural holistic healing alternative therapies for prevention, wellness and overcoming certain health conditions.

7. Need to enhance our diet through herbs/vitamins/minerals.

8. Holistic healing natural therapies handle many problems. Use for prevention, wellness and overcoming certain health conditions.

9. Use drugs and/or surgeries as a last resort or for emergency care intervention

Aberrant Thinking

10. Drugs and surgery are the salvation of modern man. They are safe and effective.

11. Surgery will handle most problems.

12. Healing comes from outside the body—drugs.

13. Chiropractic for back or neck pain only.

14. Vitamins/minerals/herbs are a waste.

15. We get all the nutrients we need in our foods.

16. Chiropractic doesn't work (it's invalid)

17. Acupuncture/magnetic therapies and other alternative healing methods don't work and have no place in healthcare— quackery!

18. No comprehension of nutritional supplements or why anyone would use them.

19. Use Vitamin C and nutritional supplements when sick with the flu or common cold.

20. Eat, drink, smoke without regard to consequences. Don't ever need a doctor etc., etc.

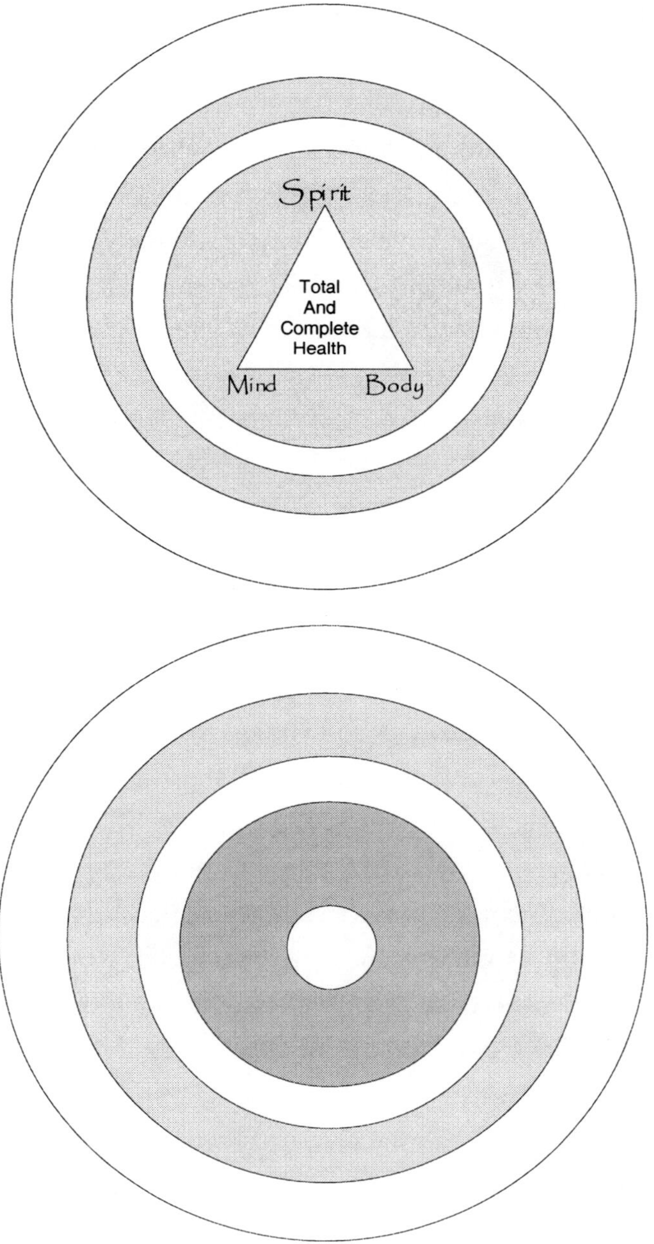
Spirit
Total
And
Complete
Health
Mind
Body

Just as people need chiropractic and the proper herbs and vitamins to enhance their nervous system, they need the proper fuel in their bodies to sustain life and to allow the body to function properly.

Toxins, bacteria, allergies, etc, inundate us. Dr. Marshall Mandell is a retired physician, author, and lecturer. He is the former Medical Director of the New England Foundation for Allergy and Environmental Diseases. I was fortunate to be in a conference where I sat next to Dr. Mandell and his son, who is a chiropractor.

Dr. Mandell told a story about a young girl he had treated. She was a very intelligent teenager with excellent grades and model behavior. Just the type of child everyone would hope for. Unfortunately, at one point in her schooling a great change came over her. The teachers noticed that after returning from the restroom one day, the girl acted totally out of character. She became moody, withdrawn, and difficult to handle. She would not do her schoolwork. They suspected that she had started taking drugs.

Teachers watched her, checked her locker for drugs, and alerted her parents. Everyone noticed the dramatic change in this girl and she totally denied any involvement with drugs. Her mother took her to doctors but to no avail. Finally, she was taken to Dr. Mandell. What he found was amazing!

This girl was having a severe reaction to the chemicals that were being used in the school's lavatory. The usual disinfectant had been changed to a different one than normally used. When the girl went to the lavatory she would walk in one person and out as another! Dr. Mandell even found that these chemicals were extremely hazardous to health—they were labeled as carcinogens. The school was alerted, they changed the products being used, and the girl reverted back to her usual happy, model teenager. This story illustrates the extreme reactions people can have to environmental toxins. But what about all the other students who did not have such severe reactions? Perhaps they would be labeled with A.D.D. and put on Ritalin. Perhaps they had to undergo psychological evaluations, were thought to be liars, slow learners, inadequate, and/or rebellious.

The power of this story is to be alert to our surroundings and be watchful of what we inhale, ingest, and put in our bodies. Chemicals, all chemicals, are dangerous and do not belong in our bodies. Whether they are in the foods we eat as preservatives or dyes, or whether they are drugs we think we need to cope with life or illnesses. They are all dangerous and do harm. The harm can be immediate or slow. But the one thing you can say with all certainty is that they will harm you. It is only a matter of time.

Therefore, any time you have the opportunity to handle health concerns naturally, the better your entire existence will be! It is amazing to see the extent of conditions that can be handled when diet is evaluated, harmful or allergic foods removed, and vitamins/minerals and herbs are supplemented. Or when environmental and dietary chemicals are eliminated. Conditions such as chronic fatigue, arthritis, headaches, colitis, irritable bowel, hyperactivity, learning disabilities and a host of others can be effectively treated, managed, or eliminated naturally! God has shown us the way in the Bible to heal naturally. Other ancient writings like the Auyervedic have taught the same. Isn't it about time we stopped dismissing these truths and listened to their wisdom?

"...know the truth and the truth shall set you free".

-John 8:32

My suggestion is that you become a bull's eye in terms of natural healing—get away from the drugs and the medicine cabinet. Incorporate natural healing methods like massage, acupuncture, and chiropractic into your lifestyle! Destroy the medicine cabinet. Create an herbal cabinet for your health. Target colds, flu or other problems as they may arise. Supplement a daily regime of herbs and nutrients to sustain your body and elevate your health. Eat more fruits, vegetables and drink more water! Become less susceptible to outside destructive forces.

Most people finally understand the sound reasoning and sense to exercising and eating the proper nutritious foods (although it was not that long ago that people did not understand). Most, now comprehend that exercise is not just something to be done when you are a kid in P. E. class. It is a lifetime affair and enhances your life, for your entire life. Just as people should exercise until the day they die, so too should they see a chiropractor, so too should they fuel their bodies properly, so too avoid excessive fats, pollution, and toxins. The fact is, with greater global industrialization, it becomes increasingly hard to find the raw, highly vital plants and vegetables needed to sustain us. Therefore, supplementation with herbs and vitamins/minerals is essential.

If we do nothing but supplement drugs or chemicals whether over-the-counter or prescribed, then we are actually killing ourselves. We are destroying our own health, lives and our children.

"Eighty percent of all disease is caused by trying to eliminate disease".

-World Health Organization

Are you aware of some of the statistics on drugs? Did you know the most recent landmark study of all time found that over 106,000 people die each year due to properly prescribed medications, and another 2 million become extremely ill? This does not account for over-the-counter medications, or improperly prescribed medications, and is just in the United States alone! What could the numbers in the rest of the world be? Can you imagine a city the size of Houston, Texas with half of its population becoming seriously ill and another 100,000 plus dying? That's incredible to think about.

Do not ever be lulled into the false sense of security that drugs are okay and they are the miracle to health. It is a lie. It is the lazy way out. We all want the instant cure, but this is not reality. Not with drugs and not with surgery. The only instant cure is God's cure.

Never give up. If you are selling health products, continue. Never doubt yourself, your products, or your belief. You are doing more good by introducing yourself, your family, and friends to herbs than one hundred medical doctors prescribing drugs.

"More Americans are hooked on drugs by their physicians than all the pushers on the street. It is estimated that one billion prescriptions are written in the United States every year".

-Robert Mendelsohn, M. D.

50 Million Unnecessary Prescriptions

Written each year by U. S. Doctors

(This according to U.S. Center for Disease Control and Prevention)

17 million alone to treat the common cold

Source: American Medical News; Health Watch, Volume 41, No. 21

Instead of exposing yourself to harmful toxic and perhaps unnecessary medications, consider a new and improved way to handling health concerns.

This could be your new paradigm of health and healing!

- Prevention, wellness and maintenance of a balanced body through or by choosing natural healing methods first and before medications or surgeries.

- Use of medications or surgeries when other natural means have little effect. Or emergency intervention.

- Use of natural healing methods in conjunction with drugs when drugs become necessary) to overcome the toxic effects of the drugs, and enhance the natural healing abilities of the body.

- Surgery—absolutely the last resort—for emergency intervention or the body has become damaged beyond repair.

"When you do what you love and love what you do, you experience the feeling of true worth and you magnetically attract the people, places, things, ideas and events to help you fulfill your purpose in life."

-John De Martini

Chapter 7

The Time Is Ripe For A Naturally Healed World

Now is the time, an incredible time to be involved in the natural health care business. The Nutrition Business Journal estimates that Americans spend 4.5 billion dollars each year on herbal and botanical supplements. Conservative out-of-pocket expenditures for alternative medicine in 1997 was 27 billion dollars!

Herbs have been used since the beginning of time to heal, in ceremonies, in rituals for healing, and to ward off evil. And although herbs are no longer used for sacrifices, they have become a wonderful source for healing in our modern world. We are finally evolving to the point where some of the old ways do not seem so primitive, ignorant or bizarre and they can be embraced and appreciated for their merits. Although, many allopathic physicians (medical doctors) still reject natural medicine, science has evolved to the point of proving and validating that thousands of years old remedies do, in fact, work and are efficacious.

For example, did you know that under the Chinese Emperor, Shen Nung, the Materia Medica documented the benefits of eating soy? This was recorded in 2838 B. C.! We now can document that adding soy to the diet may reduce the risk of heart disease. Five thousand years ago, a great sage of India wrote Vedas in the original Sanskrit language. Many people are now becoming aware of the rebirth of the ayurvedic methods. They employ systems of natural healing through the use of plants and balancing the body. Ayurveda means “the science of life”.

Now, for the first time, there is a large portion of the scientific community, doctors of chiropractic, naturopaths, herbologists, acupuncturists, etc. and an increasingly aware population searching for answers. These groups of people are now in tune and linked with our highly technologic era. We can find answers. Now, as never before, we have the ability to test, improve, analyze, and synergize herbs and natural supplements because of our great technological advancements. We are living in an era of phenomenally rapid growth and progress. Scientific equipment is improving daily. For the most part, people no longer need be watchful or skeptical about the quality of herbs. Or ask questions like, “Where did it come from? Was it a dark back room in some dingy herbal shop? How do we know what is in this product? Is it really what it is portrayed to be?”

Labs and manufacturers are hiring the best and brightest people for research and development. Many companies are taking responsibility for producing superior high quality products like guaranteed potency herbs. We can not all grow our own products and even if we could, they would not be as good as what is now being produced. Nor could we combine herbs for a powerful synergistic effect.

How safe are herbs really? Well, Michael Murray, N. D. in his book, "The Healing Power of Herbs", said the following: "In a June 1992 article appearing in the Food and Drug Law Journal, the results of an extensive review on herbal safety, (conducted by the Herbal Research Foundation, a non-profit organization whose members include experts on pharmacognosy, pharmacology, and toxicology), confirmed the lack of substantial evidence that toxic reactions to herbal products are a major source of concern. The review was based on reports from the American Association of Poison Control Centers and the Centers for Disease Control (Atlanta, GA).

Although numerous herbs growing in the wild can cause significant toxicity, the herbs commonly used in the United States for health purpose are usually safe".

It is important to note that not all nutritional products are created equally. So be informed about the products you are buying, selling, and using. Read and research as much as possible to empower yourself on the products. Michael Murray's book is a great choice as are many others.

Did you know that Paracelsus who is considered the father of pharmacology (pharmaceutical medicine) said, "That all things that man needs to remain healthy, can be found in nature, it is the job of science to find them".

The Materia Medica were books written about herbs describing them and their usage. "The Materia Medica recorded in ancient China, Babylon, Egypt, India, Greece, and other parts of the world strongly suggest that herbal medicine was highly respected in ancient times".

Plants used for healing were thought to be instinctual. Just as animals have always used plants knowing which were harmful and which were healing, so too, did humans. They did it by instinct, by tapping into that innate ability to know. They allowed God to guide them to discover the properties of all plants, which were of benefit to him.

"It was commonly believed that plants had been signed by the Creator with some sort of clue that would indicate its therapeutic use. This concept was commonly referred to as the Doctrine of Signatures". Michael Murray, N. D. describes a few common examples: "Panax ginseng, whose roots bears strong resemblance to a human figure and whose general use is as a tonic; blue cohosh, whose branches are arranged like limbs in spasm, indicating its usefulness in the treatment of muscular spasm; blood root, whose roots and sap are a beautiful blood color corresponding to its traditional use as a 'blood purifier'; lobelia whose flowers are shaped like a stomach, corresponding to its emetic qualities; and golden seal, whose yellow-green root signifies its use in jaundice as well as infectious processes". All of these uses have been confirmed by recent research.

God did not abandon us to life on this planet without the benefit of being able to utilize its resources. He obviously gave us the means to heal. Through nature, we have a tremendous resource for health and healing combined with the body's innate ability to heal and be superior to disease. We can achieve a never before realized state of health and even be healed by morning.

How can this be achieved? Simply by having enough compassion for your fellow man to share natural health with them. It may be hard, you may be rejected, you may be labeled as a quack or a charlatan. But I think in today's world, you will find more people that are receptive and searching for the truth, for compassion and answers to ill health, disease prevention and longevity.

My mother was perceived as a quack for years. I think my mom subscribed to the original "Prevention Magazine". This magazine deals with health and nutritional supplement issues. She was doling out vitamins and minerals way before it was remotely popular. Some of my relatives could not understand or did not even try to listen to the benefits of taking nutritional supplements. My mother and father are 76 and 77 respectively and very healthy. They take no medications. They have been doing this for over 30 years.

When my mom was a young girl, she remembers her mother treating her with chamomile tea due to its calming and relaxing effects, fennel and caraway water for cramping, and parsley in broth. But what really started her on taking nutritional products and doing research on her own was because of an episode that landed her in the hospital. I recall my mother spending a week in the hospital when I was young. But, of course, I did not understand it then.

My mom had a few cups of coffee with my father before he went to work. Not long afterwards, a girlfriend came to visit my mom and they talked over coffee.

About 1 o'clock that day, she experienced severe lower abdominal pains that radiated into her stomach. She, of course, went to the doctor because of its severity. While there, she began vomiting, experiencing diarrhea, and terrible pains. The doctor immediately sent her to the hospital for further testing. She recalls the doctor wanting to operate on her though he did not know what was wrong with her. This is called an exploratory surgery! Thankfully, a specialist was consulted who wanted to run some additional tests, wait, and see. They performed x-rays and barium studies to visualize the g. i. tract. They were unremarkable...nothing found! Following this, a nurse happened to notice that my mother's abdomen was bloated and hard. After inquiring, she found that my mother had not received an enema following the barium study.

The nurse said, "You always have to have an enema after being given barium. In my country, enemas are always given after barium". She was from Iran. Barium can get hard as cement and stay in the intestines. Thank God for nurses! As each day passed, the pain lessened, but my mother still experienced pain. She was given the usual unhealthy hospital meals to eat, and with each daily breakfast, a cup of coffee. My mother left the hospital without any answers to her problems.

After approximately one week, she returned to her

doctor for a follow-up visit. During their conversation, he found out that she was drinking coffee which, of course, is loaded with caffeine. The day she experienced the pain, she had drank nine cups of coffee. Upon finding this out, the doctor was alarmed and said, "This is what caused your pain. You should not drink coffee—caffeine is no good for you".

The problem had never fully resolved because each day the hospital was giving her more coffee! (I would like to know why the doctor never figured this out on the first day instead of sending her to the hospital.) My mother experienced considerable pain, many doctor visits, one week in the hospital, loss of time and money, all to find out that her body could not handle that much caffeine! The good that has come out of that horrible experience, however, cannot be measured. She stopped drinking caffeine, started researching different nutritional supplements, and started herself and her family on a road to a healthy existence. Thank you, mom! She and my father are now reaping the rewards of spending years properly caring for their health with nutritional supplements, as are their children. And those who love them are reaping the rewards of having them in their lives.

It is hard to believe that a tiny seed planted in the ground, can one day become a mighty tree bearing much fruit. We cannot always see the immediate benefit from taking vitamins, minerals, or herbs. But, it will become abundantly clear in our future! Only you can make your future a healthy one or an unhealthy one. The choice is yours, it is all up to you!

My mother was sharing her thoughts with those around her about the things she read and believed in a time when it was very unpopular to do so. But she did it anyway and is a testament to the power of nutritional supplements to aid in health and healing. I can recall many times when my mother tried to change a friend's or relative's mind on nutrition and she was turned away. Her words fell on deaf ears, and she was treated as though it were all foolishness. Now some of those people that felt that way are deceased or very ill. My parents look 20 years younger than they actually are and have no health complaints nor do they take medications. How many others in their late 70's can say that!?

Today people are much more accepting of nutritional products. Though unbelievable as it may seem, there still are the skeptics, doubting Thomases and the ones that are just too stubborn to confront the truth, as it slaps them in the face. But, in general, people are now receptive and open to alternative ways of healing and they are eager to learn more. They are educating themselves by reading, searching the Internet, and continually seeking out other's opinions. Share your knowledge and your opinions with others. It is easy!

All you have to do is just share the benefits of the products you have used for yourself. Just as you would share about a great movie you watched, or a restaurant you enjoyed dinner in, etc.!

After all, the health of the planet depends on us all. In the United States, there are only about 55,000 chiropractors, 1,500 naturopaths, and even less homeopaths, acupuncturists and clinical nutritionists. However, there are 849,000 medical doctors prescribing drugs! Yet there are millions of people in the U.S. and six billion in the world. Can you imagine if everyone were taking herbs and natural supplements? You would see an amazing change in the world! The health of the planet would be elevated! We would evolve into a new glorious, never before realized era of health! We would have few drugs—they wouldn't be needed. Medical doctors would be needed for emergency care, trauma, and serious life threatening situations beyond the ability of natural means to handle. Our bodies would achieve a higher level of existence of health and immunity, with the ability to handle stresses, (outside, external interference) without crashing. Increased health means happier people. Happier people without pain make friendlier and more loving people. Tolerance for each other improves and goes beyond tolerance to comradeship. People's hates prejudices and misconceptions disappear. Fighting stops, wars cease, pollution ends! Ultimately, we arrive at a higher state of consciousness and awareness where peace actually does exist.

It is a big vision. It is a continuum of positive cycles of action that ultimately lead to an altered state of existence that all humanity benefits from. Finally, a world that we can be proud to leave to our children! Is it worth taking natural supplements for you? Is it worth reaching out to a family member or friend and saying, "Here, you have got to try this, it may change your life!" Is it worth feeling perhaps a little discomfort and possible rejection to reach out, to step outside of your comfort zone and save the planet?

I say, "Yes!" What about you?

I am reminded of a movie, in which one incredibly courageous woman truly stepped outside of her comfort zone to effect a change. Her purpose was so strong and focused, that it enabled her to challenge herself and others. The movie is called, "The Inn of the Sixth Happiness", based on the novel, "The Small Woman", by Alan Burgess. The movie is the story of the life of Gladys Aylward and was played by Ingrid Bergman.

Gladys Aylward was "dedicated to the simple and rare belief that we are all responsible for each other". Ingrid Bergman portrays this selfless English servant who is on a mission to live with and help the people of China. Her goal is to spread the word of God through Christianity.

She sets out with a strong purpose, and against huge and many obstacles, sees her purpose through. She has a greater good in mind and allows nothing to deter her. The impact she made on those lives she touched is non-measurable.

During one particular scene, Ingrid Bergman makes the statement that she is "making each man know that he counts whether he believes in Christ, Buddha, or nothing' Although her message for the people was to teach the word of God, she had to live the word of God first. She loved them, fed them, sheltered them, saved them from aggression by the hands of foreign soldiers, and even adopted them. She made no distinction between young and old, prisoner or free man, woman or man, Buddhist or atheist, rich or poor, white skin or yellow skin. She loved them all equally and ministered to them equally. It was not by her words, but by her deeds that she made the greatest impact.

"If one of you says to him, 'Go, I wish you well; keep warm and well fed'; but does nothing about his physical needs, what good is it? In the same way, faith by itself, if it is not accompanied by acting is dead"

-James 2:16,17

I also feel a sense of greater purpose. Let me explain...

As an adolescent, I experienced severe knife-like back pain with episodes of immobility, which ultimately turned into chronic pain. The medical doctors couldn't diagnose it and therefore, said it was growing pains and it would go away. It didn't. As an adult, I turned to a chiropractor for help. He diagnosed my condition as an undetected childhood disease. A disease, which showed no outward signs, but lay hidden in my spine, distorting it. The chiropractor confirmed what I had felt all those years, eased my suffering, improved my health and changed my life. I am eternally grateful to him and to God. It is now my turn to do the same for others. I am compelled to share my gift of chiropractic healing with others.

My purpose, therefore, is to serve humanity by sharing chiropractic healing with every person possible. Through lectures, writing of articles and books, and through my treatments, I will strive to impart knowledge and healing. I am determined to educate the world about non-drug alternative approaches to health, healing and reaching our full human potential.

Further, I will enlighten people to the absolute benefits of chiropractic health care, whether they are suffering from pain or not. As true health cannot be, and should not be, determined by one's symptoms of pain. To increase their understanding of the life changing benefits of an improved, fully functional, nervous system which can be realized through chiropractic intervention. Whether they are 1 day old or 101 years old, everyone can benefit from a fully functional nervous system!

To serve the underprivileged through medical missionary work providing chiropractic care, thereby allowing them to achieve never before realized levels of health.

Purpose then can have enormous consequences for your self and humanity. The willingness to fulfill your purpose has to be strong.

So you see, one person, changing the health of one other person has an effect that is exponential in magnitude.

One man urged me to see a chiropractor. One chiropractor improved my health and urged me to become a chiropractor. As a chiropractor, I have now helped thousands of people with their health problems. This has had a positive and powerful impact on their lives and their families lives. They have referred others to receive chiropractic care from myself and other chiropractors. One man urged me to write a book about chiropractic, I did. It has helped countless people. As patients send copies of the book to friends and family and I hear that they are now receiving chiropractic care, I am elated. One of my patient's sons has just become a chiropractor because he saw the impact chiropractic made in his mother's life. Four years later, he is now a doctor and ready to help others to heal. Now he will touch thousands of lives.

One woman came to me with ringing in her ears. Her health was so changed that she made a decision to become a chiropractor. She is now enrolled in her science classes. With the grace of God, she will become another chiropractor and touch thousands of lives. I had an idea for another book, this book, and with the support of friends and family and the grace of God, it has been published, and it is being read. Perhaps this will change your life and another and another. They will change another and another, until thousands and millions and billions of lives will be changed for the good. So you see, you never know what one thought, suggestion, or urging to another can do. One man, one woman can further alter the face of the planet. Can you be that one? Yes, you can!

This book, as well as my first book, **"Dare to Break Through the Pain,** ***A Guide to Eliminating Back and Neck Pain Naturally Without Drugs or Surgery!"*** is helping me to fulfill my purpose.

"I thank Christ Jesus our Lord who has given me strength that He considered me faithful and appointing me to His service".

-I Timothy 1:12

I believe each one of us has a great purpose within us. We just have to see it, touch it, feel it and grab hold of it. It has to be acknowledged.

At this point, I ask that you take a moment to really let what I have written effuse into your soul. Let your innateness have it for a moment. See if you can feel the truth and the relevance of what has been written so far. Acknowledge it not only on a conscious intellectual level, but also on a subconscious, reactive mind level.

This may be a good spot to re-evaluate or re-enforce your own purpose. If you have never defined your purpose, this would be a perfect time for you to do that. Write down those things that define you. Look inside yourself, reach down and with clarity, and define what your purpose in life is. You can have several purposes, but what is that one thing that with clarity, you can say consumes you, gives your life hope and definition? Write it on the following lines:

____

____

____

____

____

____

Reflect on this. Re-word until it says exactly what you want it to say. Work it and re-work it like a piece of clay until it becomes the perfect image of what you want it to be. It is your creation and the creation is you. Your spirit will guide you if you let it flow freely. Your purpose is you and therefore, is an image of you, that you want others to see, to believe, to have trusted in. It defines you at a certain point in your life.

Strength, courage, good deeds, and love, these are the things that create change. The actions of people who love you speak volumes. These are some of the gifts that were given to me by my parents. They started me on the road to where I am now. The road to health, the road to enlightenment and the road to helping others heal. If I do no more than save one person's life through the power of chiropractic, through something I said, or something I've written, then I should be able to be fulfilled. However, my goal is to do more.

If you don't change any other lives, but those in your family, you have accomplished greatness and a place of honor in the universe. However, I have confidence you will change many lives and ultimately change the face and health of the planet.

"Commit to the Lord whatever you do, and your plans will succeed".

-Proverbs 16:3

Purpose

Suddenly things snap into focus.

I've been pursuing unity all my life,

But could only glimpse the monstrous vision in fragments;

It has haunted me for years.

Each time I sighted it, I struggled to make it concrete.

At first, it seemed I only had a sculptor's

yard of unfinished figures–

Then it slowly began to make sense,

Gathered from glimpses and inferences.

More and more, this mysterious life comes together.

It may take years more to reveal the whole.

That's all right.

I'm prepared to go the distance.

-TAO 365

I have never felt a greater sense of purpose and peace in the world as I do now that I am a chiropractor. The ability to touch a person's life and change it for the better (enhance it) is a highly humbling yet rewarding emotion. Anyone who has ever helped someone heal, saved someone's life, aided the poor and hungry, helped someone else achieve success, knows exactly what I mean. I cannot dream of not being able to lay my hands on someone's spine and watch their life force turn on. It is incredible! Most people will never personally experience that sensation. So it is vague and unfamiliar and therefore may sound strange to you. Perhaps even frightening or mystifying. Much like trying to explain the ultimate beauty and grandeur of the natural world to someone who is blind and has never seen. How do you relay the emotions, the sensation of seeing a magnificent sunrise or sunset? It is impossible. It has to be experienced first hand.

But there is an opportunity for those not called specifically to a ministry or vocation of healing. That opportunity is one of changing a life of a person and the world through the use of herbs and nutritional supplements. Those of you who sell natural supplements can feel all those things I mentioned. You do not have to be a doctor or priest, social worker, missionary, etc.

Once you change one life, you will understand completely and I guarantee you will be rewarded.

"Give and it will be given to you. A good measure pressed down, shaken together and running over, will be poured into your lap.

For with the measure you use, it will be measured to you".

-Luke 6:38

"There are different kinds of
gifts, but the same spirit.
There are different kinds of
service. Now to each one the
manifestation of the spirit is given
for the common good. To one
there is given through the Spirit
the message of wisdom, to another
the message of knowledge by
means of the same Spirit, to
another faith by the same Spirit,
to another gifts of healing by that
one Spirit..."

-1 Corinthians 12:4-10

Chapter 8

Could You Be One Of God's Healers?

"Each patient carries his own doctor inside him, they come to us not knowing that truth. We are at our best when we give the doctor who resides within each patient a chance to work".

-Albert Schweitzer, M.D.

What is the definition of the word doctor? It means to try to heal, to mend. It is from the Latin meaning teacher. To me, this means that every human being should be considered, and consider themselves a doctor!

I would like to suggest that every one of us is a doctor and a physician for ourselves, our families, and for mankind. Not only is it our right to be able to share valuable knowledge about health and healing, but I feel it is a responsibility. It is a responsibility to care for our fellow man. All societies throughout time, all religions have echoed a basic premise that tells us we are all in this life together and we must nurture and care for each other and if we do, we will be rewarded. The Bible tells us:

"When the Son of Man comes in His glory...the King will say to those on His right, 'Come, you who are blessed by my Father; take your inheritance, the kingdom prepared for you since the creation of the World. For I was hungry and you gave me something to eat. I was thirsty and you gave me something to drink...I was sick and you looked after me'.

-Matthew 25:31-36

He didn't say when I was sick, you brought me to an apothecary, a doctor, or H. M. O. No! He said you cared for me. Now I'm not saying don't seek the help of a physician when needed and I'm not suggesting for you to attempt to prescribe medicine. Although, lay people do this each and every day. Have you ever heard anyone say, "Oh, you have a headache, go get some Tylenol"? Or, "You have an upset stomach, go try some Maalox"? People who do this aren't actually trying to prescribe medicine. No, their basic human instinct to help a fellow human is coming out, emerging, and breaking forth. They feel through some knowledge that they might hold or through a personal experience they have had, that they owe it to this individual to share their little secret of healing. Hasn't everyone at one time or another done this for another?

Jesus is telling us that every human life is the responsibility of the other humans. Because, in fact, we are all one. Not taking care of another is an injustice. It is a shirking of one's duty and it is immoral. It would be no different than pretending that certain parts of your body did not, in fact, belong to the whole of the body. Or believing that your feet or ears were somehow less significant than the other parts of you. Therefore, they shouldn't be given as much attention or be properly taken care of; or when damaged in some way, just ignored because they were considered unimportant to begin with. No! Every single cell and tissue of our bodies are, in fact, related to us, tied to us in some cosmic universal way. And just as you care for every part of your body, so should you care for every other living being on this planet.

"For we were all baptized by one Spirit into one body—whether Jews or Greeks, slave or free- and we were all given the one Spirit to drink".

-I Corinthians 12:13

Our body parts are sacred and should not be drugged, abused, cut out and removed unless absolutely necessary. When everything else has been tried and all other means exhausted. Jesus clearly showed us in I Corinthians:

"The body is a unit though it is made up of many parts; and though all its parts are many, they form one body...if one part suffers, every part suffers with it; if one part is honored, every part rejoices with it. Now you are the body of Christ, and each one of you is a part of it".

-Corinthians 12:12-27

Therefore, I invite you to think differently about your role in the healing of the planet. If you merely take herbs for yourself, do more! Share it with others. If you sell herbs, do it with passion and enthusiasm. It is a universal concept that we must heal each other in mind, body, and spirit.

I am reminded of the movie, "Schindler's List". Hopefully, you've seen it. But if you haven't, make a note to yourself now to rent it. You'll be glad you did. It is an incredible film that I believe should be required viewing for every human being. But make sure you have a lot of tissues with you. The movie depicts the beginning of World War II, when the Nazis invaded Krakow, Poland. They rounded up all the Jews and were systematically eliminating them.

The story is about the tragic and horrific events of one group of people attempting to extinguish an entire race. Through this darkness, one man emerged to take a stand against it. This man was Oskar Schindler. A member of the Nazi party, a businessman, an opportunity seeker. He went to Krakow specifically to make money from the war. At first, he was indifferent to the pain and suffering that was all about him. But as events continued to worsen and he witnessed the casual murder of human beings, he was forced to face the reality that was so horrible. No longer could he ignore the plight of the people who were working in his factory. The total humiliation and suffering that was perpetuated to the Jews around him. It was the essence of pure evil. Humans that were treated as less than animals and then exterminated as one would do to an unwanted insect.

A Jew, Itzhak Stern, was Schindler's accountant and really started the work of saving his comrades lives. In my mind, Schindler may never have come to the point of helping these people without him. But eventually, he did all that was in his power to save these people. He created a list of names of his workers and paid to save their lives. The end of the movie is touching. Germany has surrendered and the Jews are free. Schindler's workers donate the gold from their teeth to make a ring for him in gratitude for saving their lives. The inscription reads in Hebrew from the Talmud, *"Whoever saves one life, saves the World entire".*

Schindler saved 1,100 Jews, but as the movie depicts, he was broken- hearted, and crying because he felt that he didn't do enough. A gold pin he still had could have paid for one more Jew. The car he had might have bought ten. Though he felt he hadn't done enough, those 1,100 lives he saved turned into over 6,000 descendants, with countless more to follow!

I believe this man, who wrongly felt guilt and remorse invalidated all the good he had done. He took on tremendous guilt that did not belong to him. But, his emotion and passion for his purpose of saving these Jew's lives were so great that it consumed him.

How many of us will be able to say at the end of our lives, that we saved 1,100 lives? And in reality, much, much more because countless generations will be feeling the ripple effect of this man's great deed as yet generations and generations are born from his selfless act of compassion?

We may never have an opportunity to work on that grand of a scale. And hopefully, the world can begin to learn from devastating events like those and prevent and never repeat them.

Can we ever imagine the extent of the good that we do when we help one human being?

Don't take your role in life lightly. Don't ever believe that one person can't make a difference—you can!

But, as I have mentioned before, if you only influence, change or save but one life, you have accomplished a monumental success. Therefore, don't be afraid of rejection, don't succumb to fear of rejection. Boldly go about life, telling of the wonders of natural healing, telling others of herbs, chiropractic, acupuncture, massage, homeopathy, Qigong and of magnetic therapy. When you see someone bent over in pain, or with the flu, reach out to him or her and let them know that there are natural ways to heal. When you see someone about to take a drug or they are standing in the pharmacy line or looking at those non-prescription drugs, let them know that there is a better way, a natural way, God's way. Whether they are a Christian, Jew, Buddhist, Muslim, etc., we are all part of a bigger plan of life. Everyone may not agree on the image of God. Most intelligent people can however, agree upon a higher power, a universal intelligence, a creator, and a maker that designed our planet and created our lives. Anyone who has a belief such as this owes it to all of us to heal the planet through natural means.

"He called his twelve disciples to Him and gave them authority to drive out evil spirits and to heal every disease and sickness".

-Matthew 10

I believe that it is our responsibility to follow Jesus' footsteps and become his disciples not only preaching his word, but also in providing health and healing. Even if the best you can do is to educate another person to natural healing. The use of that knowledge is solely up to them.

Again being reminded of the phrase, W.W.J.D.

"Just then a woman who had been subject to bleeding for twelve years came up behind him and touched the edge of his cloak. She said to herself, 'If I only touch his cloak, I will be healed.' Jesus turned to her and said to her, 'Take heart, daughter'. He said, 'Your faith has healed you'. And the woman was healed from that moment".

Now I am not suggesting that any of us remotely have the power that Jesus had, but I use that to show the power of faith and faith can heal. Faith in yourself can bring you great happiness and success. Faith in the healing power of herbs and the correct use of them can make them powerful. Probably everyone has heard of the placebo effect. When a simple substance (usually a sugar pill) is used and the individual is healed or overcomes some sickness. When medical doctors can show no clinical reasoning for that to work. Yet it does. Because there is power in the faith of that person who believes in that little pill the doctor gave him. Which on its own would do absolutely nothing. Can you imagine the tremendous power and ability of having faith in something like an herb or vitamin/mineral that you know actually works and has been used for centuries in healing?

"Jesus went through all the towns and villages, teaching in their synagogues, preaching the good news of the kingdom and <u>healing</u> every disease and sickness...Then he said to his disciples, 'The harvest is plentiful but the workers are few. Ask the Lord of the harvest, therefore to send out workers into his harvest field".

It is obvious that Jesus is saying that there are many people that need to be ministered to. Not only to spread the word of God, but also to deliver from illness and disease.

Jesus then, is asking all of us to be his disciples and continue his work. I believe it is our duty to show others that there is a natural way to health and healing.

"Anyone who does not take his cross and follow me is not worthy of me".

-Matthew 10:38

In his book, "The Greatest Miracle in the World", Og Mandino writes about a man named Simon Potter. Simon is what is called a rag picker. He describes it this way:

"A rag picker is one who picks up rags and other waste materials from the streets and junk heaps to earn a livelihood...however, I am not that sort of a rag picker...I search out waste materials of the human kind, people who have been discarded by others, or even themselves, people who still have great potential, but have lost their self-esteem and their desire for better life. When I find them I try to change their lives for the better, give them a new sense of hope and direction and help them return from their living death".

Why can't we be rag pickers? Why shouldn't we?

"I tell you the truth whatever you did for one of the least of these brothers of mine you did for me".

-Matthew 25:40

But why wait for these people to fail and bottom out. Before a person has been ultimately destroyed, the light of their spirit dimmed, or snuffed out, wouldn't it be better for them and for humanity if we can put some fail -safe measures in ahead of time? Keeping a person of sound and healthy body goes a long way to helping them achieve and maintain a healthy mind.

People are running, in record numbers to drugs like Prozac to help them cope with life. Can't help be given beforehand? Isn't it actually better to prevent a home from burning down than to allow it to burn completely to the ground and then work to re-build its structure and spirit? Couldn't some fail -safe measure be used to reduce the likelihood of a fire but if a fire did occur, that it could be contained and handled? Isn't it the same for a human being? Proper care of the physical, chemical and emotional aspects of a human being throughout their lifetime is more logical and easier than attempting to rebuild a destroyed life! Remember the old saying, "An ounce of prevention is worth a pound of cure".

I urge you—if you are selling nutrition, stay with it. The rewards will be astronomical. The greater good of the planet is in your hands. This is no small responsibility. Yes, you may become very wealthy doing it, or perhaps you won't, but maybe you will save one person's life. Perhaps, you will give one person the right combination of herbs that helps their cancer go into re-mission. And it will be worth it. Have you heard of the term survival value?

Survival Value. This term has been used since the early 1900's. It is based on the idea that any action has a value to it that lives on long after the action has taken place.

Elbert Hubbard said, "All worthy deeds, all honest work, all sincere expressions of truth whether by pen or by voice—have a survival value".

It is not just what we do with our lives, but the quality with which we do it. What good may come from our presence on this planet and of what value will it be to those that come after we have passed?

"Courtesy, kindness, goodwill, right intent, all add up to the sum of human happiness. Not only do they benefit the individual who gives them out, but they survive in various forms and add well being to the world. All acts whether work or play, should be judged with the idea of survival value in mind".

Healing people naturally has tremendous survival value. Introducing a person to health and healing through vitamins and herbs will change them, their family, and the world. The survival value is immeasurable!

"Health and happiness are the results of a multiplicity of thoughts and actions possessing survival value".

If there is even a remote possibility of this being true, don't you think saving a life goes a long way towards your survival value? Do you think you might be in God's favor? So do not give up. You should never give up attempting to do good for your fellow man. No matter how tough it may be at times.

Think of the enormous impact Thomas Edison had on the planet. Think how many lives he improved, enhanced, and undoubtedly saved by inventing the incandescent electric light bulb. But did you know before he perfected it; he tried more than 10,000 different ideas, all of which failed? When do we stop and give up? Some, like Edison, never give up. They never quit. They see the greater good for mankind. Winston Churchill said: "Never, never, never quit!"

L. Ron Hubbard, the researcher and developer of "Dianetics, A Science of Human Behavior", believed and wrote about the eight dynamics of life and that life is a game, the goal of which is to survive.

Og Mandino, in his book, "A Better Way to Live", also speaks of life as a game and being able to know and master the rules of the game, to live happily, have success and survive.

But, survival is more than just mere existence. Hubbard managed to break down the one dynamic of survival into actually eight different parts. Survival actually then depends upon doing the most good for the most dynamics. They are self, sex (being able to continue life), group, mankind, life, the physical universe, spiritual, and infinity (our urge towards eternal life and the Supreme Being). Thus, the more good that any of us does for each of these eight dynamics, then the better our survival. How many dynamics can you influence by keeping yourself healthy, your family healthy, sharing nutrition with strangers, helping them get well, improving their productivity, their lives, allowing them to influence others and on and on and on, spreading across the planet?

"See that you also excel in this grace of giving".

-II Corinthians 8:7

Look at what one man ultimately did to change the face of the world for good, look at how many lives he changed and saved for thousands of years. His message is short and precise.

"Love one another. As I have loved you, so you must love one another."

-John 13:34

Ask yourself this question. Do you love yourself enough to: eat healthy, put the proper nutrients in your body, exercise, and stay away from drugs? (This includes non-prescribed and prescribed drugs.) Do you love yourself enough not to be misled by propaganda, to take an affirmative stance for your health, to not follow the path of least resistance, to be open to the truth that drugs are chemicals which are toxic to the body? Do you love yourself enough to stay away from unhealthy foods like fast food, t. v. dinners, pre-packaged, pre-made foods that are filled with colorings, preservatives, and additives that make it look like food to sit on the shelf or stay in the freezer longer without spoiling?

Now if you love yourself enough, do you love the others in your family, your friends, neighbors, or coworkers?

Do you love them enough to share with them what they can be doing to lead a healthy life? Do you love them enough that when they say their child is taking an antibiotic for an ear infection, you tell them that antibiotics do not work for ear infections, that in fact, their child will be more susceptible to other health problems? That the problem is so severe that 1 in 4 children tested at Children's Medical Center was found to harbor antibiotic resistant bacteria!

Do you love them enough to tell them that super bacteria have been created by the over use of antibiotics? That you know of some good vitamins/minerals and herbs that they should take? Do you tell them to go to a chiropractor because chiropractors rid kids of ear infections all the time? To find out if their nervous systems can be enhanced to fight ill health?

Do you love people enough to follow Jesus' footsteps?

Jesus Christ saves us in more than one way. He died on the cross to save us from our sins, but, He also taught us to reach into our hearts, our souls and care for other human beings as we would love and care for ourselves.

"Serve one another in love...carry each other's burdens, and in this way you will fulfill the law of Christ".

-Galatians 5:13, 6:2

It is not enough to use alternative health yourself, to buy herbs for yourself. It is your duty and responsibility to reach out and share this message of healing with others.

Do not keep it a secret!

You may be rejected many times. You may become frustrated or want to give up. But, remember the next one that says "yes", you may just have changed their life. Og Mandino wrote the following:

"Inside every living person is a very special ingredient. We've never seen it, we've never touched it, we've never been able to locate it. But it's there—and I'm convinced that it was put there by God. We've given that special ingredient many names through the years--soul, spirit, light, flame, but what we call it is not important so long as we realize that we have it—a special gift, a gift from God...what's it worth to our world if we can rescue just one person from the misery of failure and help him or her reach full potential?"

Mother Theresa was a Catholic nun who dedicated her life to God by serving the less fortunate in India. Mother Theresa, unfortunately, died in 1998. But before she died, she had helped literally thousands and thousands of people live a better life by providing them with food, shelter and much needed medical care. Mother Theresa said that when she would serve these people, she would think that it was Christ in some terrible disguise. Can you imagine the power in that thought? If every human being you encountered, you envision as Christ, what would you do and say to help them achieve their health?

"Once you've seen the face of God, You see that same face on everyone you meet".

-365 TAO

B. J. Palmer wrote this about chiropractic. I think it is such an important idea that I have to share it with you. But the concept can be applied to herbs, nutritional products, magnets and other natural healing. It is called:

The Big Idea

A slip on the snowy sidewalk in winter is a small thing. It happens to millions.
A fall from a ladder in the summer is a small thing. It also happens to millions.
The slip or fall produces a subluxation.
The subluxation is a small thing.
The subluxation produces pressure on a nerve.
That pressure is a small thing.
That decreased flowing produces a dis-eased body and brain.
That is a big thing to that man. Multiply that sick man by a thousand, and you control the physical and mental welfare of a city.
Multiply that man by one hundred thirty million, and you forecast and can prophesy the physical and mental status of a nation.
So the slip or fall, the subluxation, pressure, flow of mental images and dis-ease are big enough to control the thoughts and actions of a nation.
Now comes a man. And one man is a small thing.
This man gives an adjustment. This adjustment is a small thing. The adjustment replaces the subluxation.

That is a small thing. The adjusted subluxation releases pressure upon nerves. That is a small thing. The released pressure restores health to a man. This is a big thing to that man. Multiply that well man by a thousand, and you step up the physical and mental welfare of a city. Multiply that well man by a million, And you increase the efficiency of a state. Multiply that by a hundred thirty million, and you have produced a healthy, wealthy and better race for posterity. So, the adjustment of the subluxation to release pressure upon nerves, to restore mental impulse flow, to restore health, is big enough to rebuild the thoughts and actions of he world. The idea that knows the cause, that can correct the cause of dis-ease, is one of the biggest ideas known. Without it, nations fall; with it, nations rise. This idea is the biggest I know of.

-B. J. Palmer, 1944

What a concept! Those of us who see chiropractic work every day to improve the health of a human being by restoring proper nervous system function, know this to be true. It is an incredible concept and it works for natural supplements and herbs too. Use of nutritional supplements can only aid in the improved functioning of the human body. This improved and healthy individual influences others and the ultimate beneficiary is mankind! Do some good for yourself and for others. Improve your health and the health of mankind.

"Do all the good you can, by all the means you can, in all the ways you can, in all the places you can, at all the times you can, to all the people you can, as long as ever you can."

-John Westley

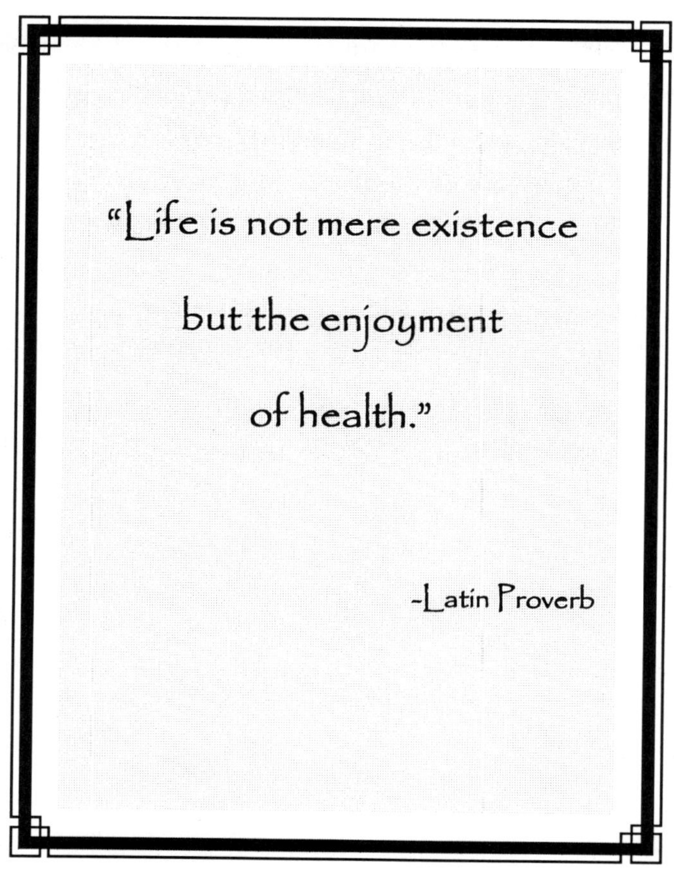
"Life is not mere existence
but the enjoyment
of health."
-Latin Proverb

Chapter 9

Eating Healthy

God speaks to us about food in the Bible. What foods to use and which to avoid. People like Dr. Reginald Cherry's, "The Bible Cure", and Reverend Malkmus', "Why Christians Get Sick", reflect on the proper foods and eating as described in the Bible. Reverend Malkmus even states that according to God's plan, people should live healthfully up until 120 years old!

God gave us the prescription for a healthy existence—which foods would aid in disease prevention, healing of ailments, and life extension. But how can we incorporate these foods into our diets today with such diversity of population spread over the globe in different environmental grouping? Much of the world's populations are city dwellers. Is it possible for these people to eat the proper foods that God prescribed? Vast majorities of people in the United States are leading, fast paced lives that seem to continue in an accelerated rate, and no one is willing to slow down.

The more technology that is developed to make our lives better, the more complex our lives become. Although there is only a certain amount of time in a day, it seems that we continually try and squeeze more and more into it. Like a Christmas stocking that is bulging from all the presents, we want to get just one more into it. We seem to be burning up time at an accelerated rate. I've noticed this in people with children. Parents eager to give their children more than they had growing up, or want or demand excellence from their children—athletically, musically, and academically. Or they want to prepare them for life to have an edge over the next person.

These well intentioned parents have their children enrolled in soccer, football, dance, gymnastics, cheer leading, Bible study, swimming, tennis, golf, karate, piano, band and the list goes on and on. Do they really have the time to eat healthy? They should, but do they? And what about the rest of the population—the corporate ladder climbers, the entrepreneurs, small businessmen and women who swear that they will one day slow down to enjoy life? How many of them are eating properly? And what about the men and women who are in health care who work long hours, graveyard shifts to keep others healthy? Have we checked their eating habits lately? Have you ever noticed many of these people are highly over weight and also smoke?

Consider the men and women who keep us safe in law enforcement and the fire department. Do they really have the ability to eat properly all the time? How about the blue collar workers, the miners, the factory workers, and the truck drivers who spend days and weeks on the road? The salesmen who travel by car from one diner or truck stop to the next. Or the businessmen who travel and rack up airline miles and are rarely home, eating airline food and hotel food? And what about the small town, rural

Americans who aren't farmers and don't grow their own food, who eat in that greasy spoon everyday with no real choice for healthy eating?

And, of course, there are the hamburger franchises and a host of other fast food restaurants that seem to be in every town in America and soon to be in a neighborhood near you throughout the world. They are there to serve you breakfast, lunch, and dinner—three non-wholesome meals a day. Or what about all those people that don't live in a trendy, upscale, higher consciousness neighborhood and don't have access to an organic health food store? I could fill pages with occupations and situations of people not able to eat properly.

What can these people do? Do they all really have the ability or equal opportunity to eat healthy, the way God designed? There are very few perfect eating situations. But even if we could slow our lives down to eat properly, could we glean out of the foods the proper nutrients that should be there? The reality to all of this is no. Are foods all they should be? This is highly doubtful—we have nutrient depleted soils that lack the vitamin and mineral content that we need to sustain us. We have mass growing of food polluted with chemicals, pesticides, and insecticides. Mass shipping and warehousing that allows the nutrients to be leached from the foods. We have livestock (cows, chickens, turkeys, and pigs) that are pumped with chemicals, steroids, and antibiotics to either ward off disease or make them plumper and juicier. And we have fish that come from waters polluted with toxic waste.

We need help and as sad as it may sound, we need to take little pills that supply what we are not getting in our foods either because it is not there or because we are not eating healthfully. But remember! Even if we choose and do eat healthy, the nutrients aren't there! One figure I read said that to get the nutritional value of one head of lettuce from 1948, today we would have to eat 20! Can you do that? I know I can't. Although God gave humanity His design for eating properly and provide for us, nutrient rich foods to sustain and keep us healthy, man has found ways to destroy His plan.

Some people truly have limited choices and others choose to be limited. But the one thing we all have in common is the fact that nutritional supplements do need to be added to our diet. This is not to say they should be substituted, for rational thought, and replace food. But the phytonutrients that God planned for us to have may now have to come in encapsulated form!

Phytonutrients are an ever-increasing incredible way to replace what's missing from our foods and target certain areas for prevention and treatment of disease!

"Stop drinking only water, and use a little wine because of your stomach and your frequent illnesses".

-I Timothy 5:23

Today many studies point to the benefits of drinking a little wine to help the heart and vascular system. Many people are becoming increasingly aware of anti-oxidants and the benefits they hold for anti-aging. Grape seed extracts are one of the best sources of anti-oxidants!

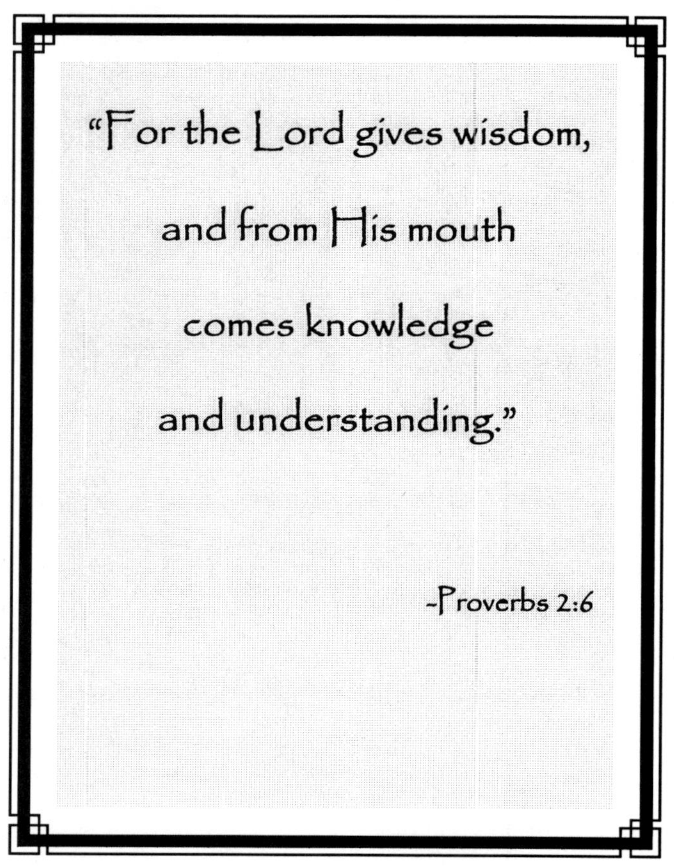
"For the Lord gives wisdom,
and from His mouth
comes knowledge
and understanding."
-Proverbs 2:6

Chapter 10

The Illusion of Health

"Sickness is felt, but health not at all".

-Thomas Fuller, M. D., 1732

This is an interesting quote, sickness is felt, but health not at all. I would like to change that quote slightly to sickness is felt, (eventually) but health not at all. Why did I put the word eventually into that line? Because the pain or symptoms of sickness may take a long time to actually show. By the time this occurs, much damage has been done to the body. Perhaps irreversible damage!

The illusion is that if we don't see or feel a sign or symptom, then we believe ourselves to be healthy. When, in fact, this can be a dangerous illusion. Although, symptoms are our bodies warning system to alert us to a potential problem, it is not an early warning system. In other words, we do not have any flashing red signals that we visualize, there are no audible warning bells or tones, and there are no little voices that call to us. Nothing tells us in gradual predetermined stages that a major health condition is the inevitable end of the destructive path of neglect and over indulgence that we are on. When our arteries become 10 percent, 20 percent, 50 percent, or 90 percent occluded we are not signaled. No, we don't get the warning until many times it is too late or there may be no recovery; such as a stroke or heart attack.

We don't get the signals that our vertebrae are irritating and interfering with our nervous system or the lack of proper nutrients is causing a 10 percent, 20 percent, 50 percent, or 90 percent nervous system shut down. Or have we possibly been neglecting some of the subtle warnings—the fatigue, the extra weight, becoming easily exhausted, having no energy or wind? Maybe we've been ignoring those thoughts like "I really shouldn't eat this", "I know I shouldn't smoke, but..." "I'll start exercising next week".

We have all heard the stories of people who looked healthy, felt healthy and then suffered a sudden death, or debilitating stroke, or even perhaps found out that they had cancer, with only a short time to live. Not only have all of us heard these stories, but also many of us have lived them either personally, or with a close family member. A mother, father, sister, brother, husband, wife, son or daughter. It is devastating to live through. But it is also a strong lesson in life that we must learn from and not ignore. Ignorance is not bliss! Illusion is dangerous. It is imperative that we not only listen to the subtle changes and impressions our bodies are giving us; but also know with certainty that there is accountability for our health choices, and gambling with our health or our loved one's health may have horrible and unacceptable consequences.

Therefore, the best type of health care is actually preventative health care. Give your body all the proper care and nutrients to keep disease at bay.

I told you my father is 77. Two years ago, he went for an annual check-up. The nurse asked him, "What medications are you taking?" His reply was, "I don't take any medications".

She asked, "How old are you?" He replied, "75". She said, "I can't believe you aren't on any medications and your blood pressure is 90 over 70. This is unheard of. What are you doing?" He replied, "Vitamins and herbs! My wife has been giving them to me for years!"

You see the average adult 60 plus is on over 10 medications. In fact, in 1991, seniors filled 650 million prescriptions! That's more than 15 per person. According to the health advocacy group, Public Citizen, 40 to 50 percent of the medications most often prescribed to our older citizens are over used, mis-prescribed or abused. When we are ill we all want to be healed by morning but drugs won't heal us. Healing must come from within our bodies and from God.

As previously spoken of, we must have faith in God, and if we truly had total unwavering faith, it is possible to be healed by morning. In fact, in truth, we could be healed now, instantaneously. But how often does that happen? God can cure us now in less time than the flash of a lightning strike. But he also gives us the power to think, to react, to reason and make choices. To use everything that he put on this planet for our health, well being, and comfort. It is all at our fingertips, at our disposal and command. It is ours to use as we see fit and to use, hopefully, with responsibility.

Unfortunately, because most of us don't walk around in a higher state of consciousness, we allow ourselves to be influenced by outside elements and because our thinking is aberrant, we leave ourselves susceptible (ripe) for diseases and viruses to attack us and actually hurt us.

But what if our minds didn't even entertain or accept the thought of ill health? Would we become sick?

"Whatever you can conceive and believe, you will achieve".

-Napolean Hill

We reap what we sow! We get in life what we believe we deserve or are worthy of, good or bad, positive or negative. Can we attain ultimate health? Many of us push our bodies so far that inevitably they break down after months or years of abuse. I see it every day in my practice. People who are so busy being busy, not taking time to get well and heal. At this point, we are fighting the old uphill battle. It is a war. Do not delude yourself into thinking it is less. We are being invaded by a foreign threat to our homeland. Where we live—our bodies! We ignore all the warning systems. The sore throat, the fatigue, the increased symptoms of stress.

And then we totally are surprised that we became sick, we have the flu or an ulcer or allergy or cancer or heart disease. Then what do we do? We still do not rest, we push on, take the drugs because they are purported to be the cure all and we do not have time to heal naturally. Or maybe some herbs are taken. But, do we take enough?

No! Just one or two magic pills. Do we do all the things necessary to fight the battle, like go to a chiropractor or try herbs, magnets, or Qigong? No! It is a war, folks. Hit it with all you got!

I am continually amazed when patients tell me, "Doctor, those herbs are expensive and I can not afford to spend $50, $100, or $200 a month on this". You can't afford not to. Your life depends on it!!! How important is that? What is your commitment to your life, to your husband, wife, daughter, or son? Give up that motorcycle, videos, boat, and gambling trip to Las Vegas, etc. Build in into your food budget. Give up the cakes, cookies, etc. The same person that says they cannot afford it, will spend $2,000 to $5,000 on a ski vacation, buy a new car, or spend $500 to $1,000 a month on entertainment, alcohol, or cigarettes. They place a higher value on every imaginable materialistic, pleasurable item than they place on their own health. How sick is that!!? What is their real priority here? What is their commitment to themselves and their families? How much more money will it cost them in the long run when their bodies or minds totally break down? How will they justify this?

When people comment that they cannot afford to take vitamins/minerals and herbs, it is because their awareness has to be elevated so they can see the benefits of using the products. The problem is not of affordability, but a problem with an individual's perception of value. They have not been given a good enough reason to take them or they have not made it a priority. These people are minimizing their problems and thereby rationalizing their unwillingness to spend money on their health. Someone needing one magic drop of a healing elixir to save his or her life would surely pay any price for it.

Some people are finicky and shortsighted. They cannot see the forest through the trees so to speak. They worry or attempt to rationalize why they cannot afford to spend an extra $100 or $200 on proper nutritional supplements or the proper diet. Yet, they do not think twice about going out to a nice restaurant and spending $100 on a meal full of fat and sugar, or alcohol; or maybe buying a new deer rifle, bass boat, ski equipment, scuba equipment, dresses, business attire, braces, etc. What is not realized is that of the small amount of money that is not spent now on proper living (preventive maintenance), will cost enormous amounts of money later when their past bad living actually catches up to them and pulls them down. It could be in the form of a mental breakdown or perhaps a physical breakdown, an illness or disease that destroys lives, destroys jobs, and puts one in the hospital and costs 5 to 10 times more or higher. Perhaps hundreds of thousands of dollars in today's health care costs will be spent! We spend thousands of dollars on our external being but how much do we actually spend on the inside to reduce the risk of damage or failure? Preventive maintenance should be done on our bodies as well as our cars.

I am reminded of a woman that I used to know. She

had an automobile that was her primary source of commuting to and from her job. Therefore, you could say this vehicle was a crucial part of her life because she depended on it to take her to work. Her existence depended upon her having a job and, of course, getting paid.

What is surprising to me is how little actual importance she placed on this vehicle or at least she showed no signs of concern. Yet her ability to getting along in life on a daily basis depended upon it. She just seemed to think the car would always be there, always working fine without even any effort or casual attention or thought from her. The problem is that her lack of attention to the car eventually confronted her with full force.

One day the engine seized on her. It would not function any longer. You see, she had not even bothered to perform the basic necessities on the vehicle, no preventive maintenance. She never added oil! An engine does not like to run without oil, in fact, it will not for very long. This casual neglect of her car's engine, now turned into a major financial crisis that threatened her normal state of existence. What could have been handled for mere pennies a day and a little time, now would cost her thousands of dollars, and create a true major financial hardship.

Human nature is to look and focus at the surface of things. We are like ostriches that stick their heads in the sand and ignore everything else or pretend it does not exist. It cannot be true because we cannot see it. People are so concerned about their outward physical appearances that they will do virtually anything to alter it, to improve it, to clothe it. People will spend thousands of dollars on tummy tucks, hair weaves, breast reduction, breast enhancement ($5,000), nose jobs, face lifts, porcelain teeth, and liposuction ($2,500 per site). Their priority is to purchase the best shirts, ties, suits, dresses, shoes, handbags, hairdos, manicures, etc. As an example, one of my patients who has a bulging disc told me he spent $5,000 to have his wife's breasts enhanced, yet he is unwilling to take the time or spend minimal dollars (less than $50 a treatment) on himself in order to heal. Even though his neglect might land him in the hospital with a $50,000 to $100,000 back surgery!

Why will we neglect our internal operating systems that support our very existence and give us life? All the expensive clothes and cosmetics will only make us beautiful corpses!

"Oh, my God! There is a blemish on my face!" But what about that blemish on our heart or that spot on our liver, or lung from too much alcohol or smoking? What about that nervous system that is compromised or the heart that is working too hard from years of abuse? What about the digestive system that has been overloaded from hard living and bad food? Isn't it time that human beings walked away from the mirror on the wall and checked the internal mirror? I think it is past time! Take a good hard look inside and correct what you can while you still can!

"The Lord does not look at the things man looks at. Man looks at the outward appearance but the Lord looks at the heart..."

-I Samuel 16:7,13

Let's take a look at a few areas that should be maintained and can add quality years to our lives!

There are three systems of our bodies that are often highly neglected and yet we have tremendous control over. These systems are the:

1. Nervous system
2. Vascular system
3. Digestive system

Each one of these systems can be very easily and properly cared for naturally. Doing so can greatly increase our health, vitality, performance, and longevity. Adversely, if they are neglected and abused, they can create massive ill health, and disease ending in needless suffering and ultimately, in an untimely death! Allow me to show you some simple diagrams to illustrate my point.

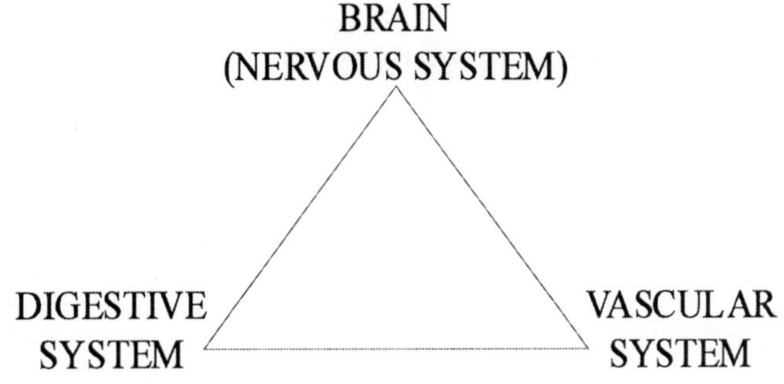

Three of the most important systems of the body in which we have great influence over as to their function and health. Balance of these systems can greatly enhance ones health, vitality, and longevity. Care for them properly and they will take care of you. Abuse them and life will be full of sickness, disease, and early retirement.

The digestive system feeds and supplies nutrients to

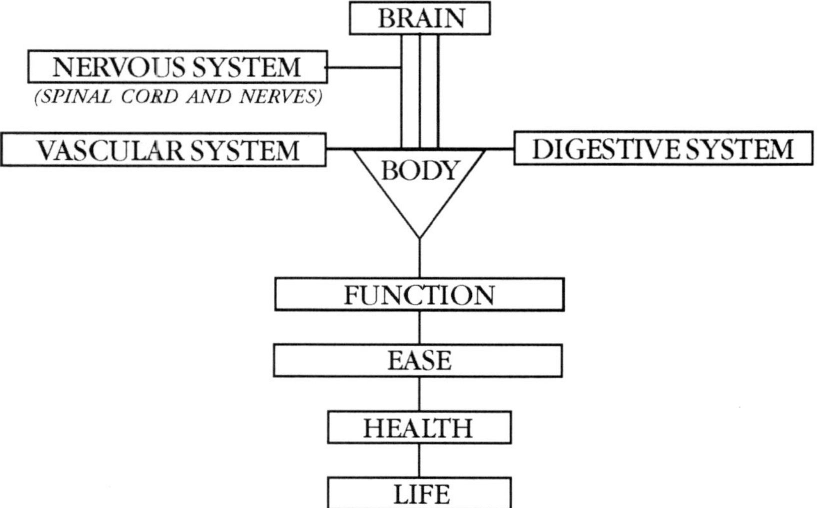

the brain and body. It is crucial to give it the proper fuel in order to receive peak performance from it. If the proper foods and nutrients are supplied, then the brain (our master control) can function properly.

If the proper fuel is put into the body, then our digestive system will allow all the nutrients to flow into our bodies-absorption. This creates proper function, the being will be at ease an experience good health and life.

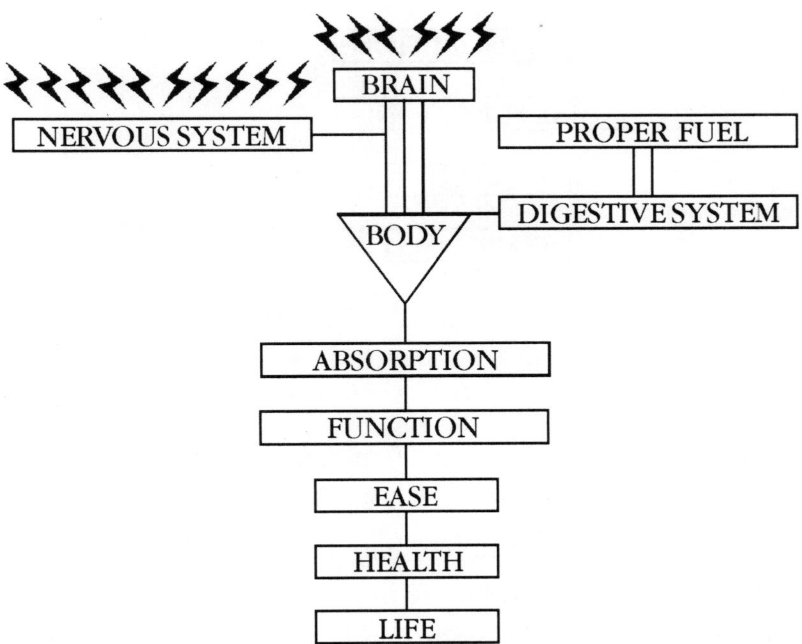

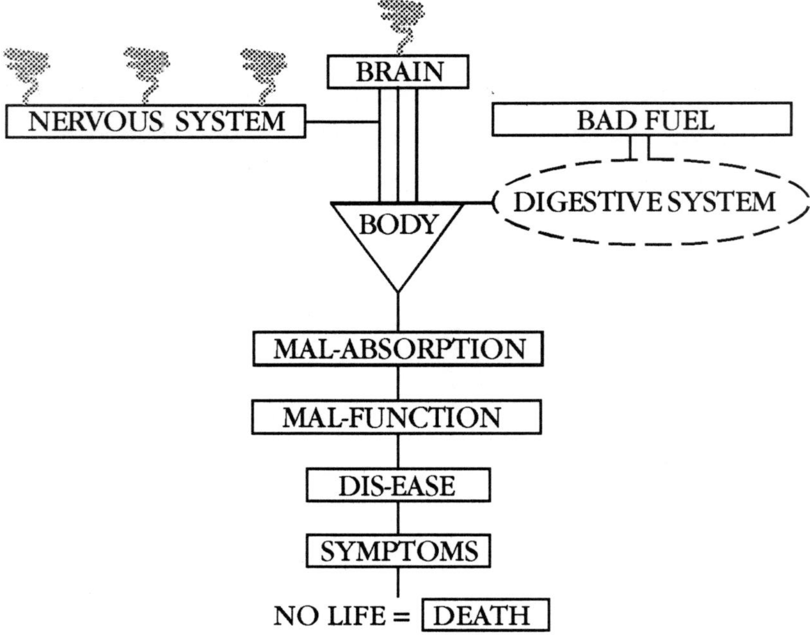

Some experts believe that 90 percent of all disease starts in the large intestine!

Putting improper or bad fuel into the digestive system can clog up the system resulting in mal-absorption. This creates malfunction of the body and brain causing further disease until symptoms are manifested. Left alone, this continues on to a non-existence state.

No Life = Death

Bad Fuel Examples = sugar, white flour, excessive salt, food additives, carbonated beverages, preservatives, fast food, cookies, cakes, alcohol, fatty or high cholesterol foods, etc., etc.

When we fuel our bodies (eat) our digestive system goes to work. It attempts to pull all the nutrients out of the fuel to feed the body and the brain (master control). Once this has been accomplished, the waste material needs to be eliminated. If it is not, the body becomes toxic, mal-functions and becomes diseased.

"Consider that you are in God, surrounded and encompassed by God, swimming in God. God's love is infinite. With God, nothing is impossible."

-Mother Theresa

Chapter 11

Deciding To Be Healthy

Ultimately, you are the only person who is in command of your life and can change its course. It's as though you were the captain of a ship with your hands on the ship's wheel. People commonly ask questions like, "When will this streak of bad luck end?" "When will I become successful?" "When will my health improve?" You are the only one who is responsible for these things, only you can command the ship to change course and turn around or take a new direction. So the question really is "Are you ready for the turning point in your health?" "Are you willing to create that turning point?" Until you are willing to create that turning point, until you firmly make that decision and are willing to take action to commit yourself to it, your health will never change.

I know many people and I am sure you know some too, in fact, you may be one that has purchased a year at the gym but never goes. Others that have purchased exercise equipment for the house, but what does it do? Sits and gathers dust or becomes a clothes tree. I know people who buy vitamins/minerals, and herbs—there they sit on the kitchen counter or in the cabinet unused or very rarely used. When I ask, "What are you taking"? They can rattle off many products. But then they tell me they do not work, so I inquire, “Really, they aren’t working for you? Well, how are you taking them and when are you taking them”? “Oh, well, I take them whenever I remember. Or once in awhile because I just hate swallowing pills”. How can any supplement possibly work if it’s not taken properly?

I find the number one reason that people do not get proper results from natural supplements is because they are not taking the products properly. There is no magic pill! Let me say it again, there is no magic pill! One, two or three does not do it. Once or twice a month does not do it. I have told people to go home and look at their supplements and tell me the expiration date on them. You cannot believe their surprise when they come back to me and tell me that they have expired and the bottle is not even empty yet! This shows you how often they are actually taking supplements. But they swear they just bought the bottle a few months ago. The second reason people don’t get results are because they are using poorly manufactured and poor quality products.

We’ve all heard it before, you generally get what you pay for. Use common sense and your own intuition about natural supplements, but also do some research on the products you are about to use. People are often misled, and blinded by price. We all want to spend as little as possible, but get the best product. The reality is that this just isn’t possible. You can’t buy a Mercedes Benz for the price of a Hyundai and you shouldn’t expect the Hyundai to perform or have the quality and features of a Mercedes Benz. You can't expect a two-dollar bottle of wine to have the same characteristics, quality, aroma and flavor of a $100 bottle of wine. Need I say more?

Not all natural supplements are in an equal playing field either. Generally speaking, buying 1000 tablets of Vitamin C for $1.99 at your super warehouse store will not be the same quality or give you the same results as Vitamin C you would buy from a superior manufacturer, found in a quality health food store or from a health care provider. This applies to vitamins or minerals as well and maybe especially herbs. Buying herbs from some drug store, street peddler, or out of a neighbor's garden will not yield the superior results as a herb that is a guaranteed potency herb. These herbs will be standardized and guaranteed to high potency levels consistent with scientific research. If you don't spend a little money and seek out the best products you will be wasting your money and suffering from the lack of effectiveness. Therefore, you might as well not take anything. It will be as effective as consuming garbage products!

The third reason is people do not understand the difference between what should be a daily dose and what would be a therapeutic dosage for a particular ailment they are trying to overcome.

To a large extent some of the pharmaceutical companies and the F. D. A. have been trying to eliminate natural supplements from the United States. In some instances, they have been successful. For example, the F. D. A. was able to remove L-tryptophan, an amino acid, from the shelves a few years ago, all under the guise of protecting the public. L-tryptophan was very popular as a natural sleeping aid. Many people are aware that turkey has high tryptophan content lending to the usual sleepiness after a large Thanksgiving meal. It had been used for years without any problems and is very safe. However, an isolated occurrence of a few deaths was all that was needed for the government to step in and eliminate L-tryptophan from consumer availability. It is my understanding that they determined the deaths were due to a bad batch of the product. But that didn't stop them from seizing control of the situation and eliminating the product in the United States.

Death on a large scale occurs daily from the use of prescription and non-prescription drugs, however, the F. D. A. is slow to act on this, if at all. Because of incidents like the L-tryptophan situation and other governmental control, natural supplement manufacturers have to be extremely careful about the claims they make about their products as well as the recommended dosages. There may be a significant difference between the recommended minimum dosage for a product and the actual therapeutic dosage needed to handle a particular ailment or condition. The majority of time I hear someone complaining that a natural supplement hasn't worked for him or her, it is due to an inadequate dosage or use of the product. So check your products, speak to an authority on the product, and do a little homework to find out what is really needed to handle a condition.

Do you want to heal? Put joy, happiness and excitement into your life? Reader's Digest has a section in the magazine that is called, "Laughter is the Best Medicine". Can this be true? Can it work? Yes, it can! A positive mental attitude, visual imagery and laughing from the heart and soul can go a long way to creating inner health. Jesus said:

"A cheerful heart is good medicine but a crushed spirit dries up the bones".

This may be a good point to talk about fear and criticism. Fear of what other people will think especially family members can create a major negative impact on our lives. Many experts talk about this, but always in terms of not being able to fulfill dreams or become a success, change jobs or change lives, take risk or start our own business. I have never heard anyone speak on the tremendously devastating effects that it can have on one's health, but it happens everyday, thousands of times a day. I especially see it very commonly in natural healing circles.

So many people who have been given misinformation, wrong data or are ignorant of a subject, transfer their beliefs or fears on to the person who wants to get well outside the traditional modes of healing. Or perhaps they explain the fact that they will be highly disappointed in you if you choose this health form or they will not support you in it because they do not agree with it.

They endeavor to make you wrong and invalidate your attempt to heal in the manner and choosing in which you so desire. Perhaps they even strive to make you feel stupid or ignorant with comments like, "It's your money!" "You are being ripped off." "If you want to flush it down the drain, it's okay with me!" "I thought you were smarter than that." "Don't be ridiculous, we're not spending money on that!" Or the dumbest one of all, "If the insurance does not pay for it, you cannot do it." "It is not covered by insurance, so I am not paying for it."

Which implies just because insurance pays go ahead and have something done whether you need it or not. And if it does not pay, you are not worthwhile enough to spend money on. Why don't you have your brain removed if insurance will pay for it?

All these types of comments serve to do is dismantle your decision to help yourself in the way you determine is best. It is done because these other people do not understand themselves and, therefore, cannot acknowledge it and put their seal of approval on it.

However, who gets hurt? That is right—you do! I know it is hard to fathom, but some people will actually let their insurance company decide the kind of care they receive. Because an insurance company will not pay, they decide not to get the help and let their health continue to worsen, all the time using the excuse they cannot afford it. Truth is, their priorities are wrong!

Some people can be very overpowering, domineering, stifling and what I would consider oppressive and abusive. I have, too frequently, seen the scenario played out. So this attitude isn't just confined to taking risks. It actually shows itself with regard to people's decisions about their own health care with husbands and wives, parents and children. I have seen when one person wants to use herbs and supplements, or chiropractic and the other is unwilling to allow the person the beingness to get the type of care they choose. However, they are too unbending and stubborn to look for truth in the situation and see the benefit. I speak briefly about this in my book, **"Dare to Break Through the Pain-** ***A Guide to Eliminating Back & Neck Pain Naturally Without Drugs or Surgery!"***

"An uneducated man lives in darkness and ignorance which creates prejudice. He is unable to relate to his surroundings, his world, his universe. He seeks approval for his actions and deeds from others and relies on their beliefs and information, to guide and direct him. He is never in control of his own heart, mind or destiny. His world becomes shaped by others without full understanding of the consequences".

As I said, I have seen this all too frequently in practice. I am reminded of a woman who became one of my best patients and achieved great health success because of her great courage. And believe me, sometimes it does take great courage to contradict the wishes of a loved one. Especially if it is a spouse and even more so if that spouse is your husband.

Let me tell you about my patient, Jenny. Jenny was suffering from severe headaches for several years and was living on medication to get through the day. She did not like or want to take the medications, however, she was not aware that there was any hope for her to correct her problem. That is until one day a friend spoke to her about seeing a chiropractor. Jenny struggled with this idea for some time, the reason why, will become clear in a moment. Finally, Jenny made the courageous decision to seek a chiropractor for help.

The chiropractor she chose turned out to be me. When she called my office and spoke to my staff she made it expressively clear that she was not coming in for an examination or treatment but only for a consultation. In fact, she made this point so strongly that my staff felt obliged to let me know of this woman's mindset. You see, it is not often that a potential patient wants to just talk. They usually want to get the help, therefore, their intention is to be examined and treated. But not this time. The consultation with the doctor was all this woman wanted. The appointment was made and kept.

Jenny came and sat in my personal office. As I inquired about her condition I asked her, "What questions could I answer to relieve your anxieties or fears?" I thought (wrongly) that she was perhaps frightened about chiropractic because of some misinformation. This was not the case. She, in fact, did want to be examined and treated if I would agree to a few conditions, and if I thought, of course, that I could truly help her with her headaches. What she was about to tell me was amazing.

Jenny's husband is a medical doctor, an internist and one of those unenlightened ones who does not understand chiropractic and therefore fears it and is prejudiced towards it. She, in fact, said that he strongly disliked chiropractors (she may have used the word hate).

In any case there is no way he would stand for her to see a chiropractor for her headaches. He would not allow it! All he would do was to prescribe Advil for her, which did not work. Jenny's decision to take responsibility for her own health was a courageous one, but one that also came conditioned. If I treated her, it had to be with ultimate discretion. My office could not have any contact with her outside the office. No phone calls to her home, no letters, and no cards. Nothing! She even said that if we happened to be in the same restaurant to please not acknowledge her. This is how fearful she was about her husband finding out that she wanted chiropractic care.

My ultimate interest was in Jenny and her health. Not in what her husband's primitive thinking was. It makes no difference to me that he does not want to understand, other than the damage it was doing to his wife and probably countless others who he kept from receiving potential help through chiropractic. However, my focus was to be about Jenny, so I agreed. I would attempt to help her heal, on her terms.

Well, it was worth it, the most beautiful thing happened. She had tremendous success in eliminating her headaches! While Jenny was in my office she read everything she could about chiropractic and natural healing. Every magazine and piece of literature on herbs. Jenny was even taking the herbs I recommended for her. However, she had to disguise them by actually putting them in her Advil bottle she kept in her purse. She dumped the Advil out and put the herbs in. That is right you guessed it, because her husband did not believe in herbs either. Can you imagine the fear she lived in about this? But, thank God she had enough strength to finally take control of her own life and get the healing she wanted regardless of what her husband thought. After all, it is her body and she was suffering.

Although she could not confront him about this, she at least had the courage to get the care, and the results were fantastic. I have had other patients who have not been so fortunate. They have not had the courage to go against the wishes of their spouse and demand the type of care they want. They believe it makes them a loyal spouse, but I believe that it makes them subservient to a dominant personality who obviously does not have their true best wishes in mind because this person is focusing on other issues such as prejudice, or money.

Mostly, I see this with men who will not allow their wives to be in control. It is sickening, sad and unbelievable in today's world. But, it continues to happen. To those of you who are women, I say take control and look after yourself, regardless of what others may believe—pray to God for help and guidance. And to the men who might be exacting this type of dominance over the woman in their lives—I say, if you love them enough—give up dominating them and let them care for their own bodies the way they please—and pray to God for forgiveness.

"The Lord does not look at the things that man looks at. Man looks at the outward appearance, but the Lord looks at the heart..."

-I Samuel 16:7,13

For the most part, I believe that men and women who get into the medical profession do it because they truly want to help another human being and effect positive changes in human life. All too often they are looking for that miracle drug that will solve it all, but actually creates more harm and destruction along the way. Doctors are being brainwashed with propaganda by pharmaceutical companies from the first day of medical school. And they are unwilling to work in harmony with other professions and ideas, to be open to the limitless potential for healing. They have been told that they hold human life in their hands and this is a powerful and awesome responsibility. They are unwilling to yield some of that power.

I am reminded of a joke in which two doctors were standing around a patient and the one doctor remarked to the other that the treatment had finally worked—they were successful! The cancer had been killed! But the other doctor remarked, "How wonderful it is, but the patient has died". This is a sad commentary. Sometimes the cure is worse than the condition in medical science. All too often the actual patient is overlooked while trying to attack the disease and condition. People have become dehumanized, pulled apart, dissected until all they are to those treating them is the actual body part, cell or condition that they are waging war against. The person is all but forgotten because the focus and attention is on treating the symptoms or disease and not the whole individual made up of spirit, mind and body.

"A woman was there who had been subject to bleeding for twelve years. She had suffered a great deal under the care of many doctors and had spent all she had, yet instead of getting better she grew worse".

-Mark 6:25

Although this occurred 2000 years ago, this kind of suffering and needless treatment still happens. We hear about it all the time, people living on high dollar medications. Sometimes it is so expensive that insurance does not pay for it. The patient can not afford it. Or people popping over-the-counter medication, like Advil, Tylenol, Ibuprofen, and others as if it were candy, totally oblivious to the severe damage they are causing to every cell of their body, destroying their kidneys and liver!

God has equipped each human being with a pair of kidneys for the purpose of removing contaminants from the blood, converting this to urine and excreting it from the body. Use of certain medications will cause eventual failure of the kidneys, requiring a person to be placed on hemo-dialysis. This is a machine that filters the contaminants and toxins from the blood the way the kidneys used to. Of course, machinery is never quite as good as our original equipment. Dialysis users can expect to be hooked up for three hours per day, three times a week.

For those people who think it costs too much for prevention or takes too much time, need only talk to a dialysis patient. The sad truth is that the majority of dialysis patients could have avoided this had they but taken care of their bodies properly with proper diet, nutritional supplementation and alternative health care when needed. Most, however, chose to seek the route of deadly drugs and masking their problems.

According to a 1999 study found on the Internet, 35 percent of the people are on dialysis due to the use of anti-inflammatories and over-the-counter medications, another 60 percent, because of prescription medications. This leaves only 5 percent because of hereditary reasons. Dialysis users are particularly vulnerable to blood infections which account for between 8 percent to 18 percent of all deaths. Wouldn't it be better to never drive your body to the point of needing dialysis?

Seemingly, a logical thinking individual might deduce that there is great danger in taking medications. And that seeking alternative solutions to health problems might be not only safer, but produce superior results. With the side benefit of actually costing a person less of what they seem to value most—time and money!

"Health in this world is the counterpart of value in Heaven. It is not my merit that I contribute to you but my love, for you do not value yourself. When you do not

value yourself you become sick, but my value of you can heal you, because the value of God's Son is one. When I said, 'My peace I give unto you', I meant it."

-A Course in Miracles

Reverend Malkmus of Hallelujah Acres writes that superior health can exist if we all practice God's natural laws. The following is quoted exactly from Revered Malkmus' newsletter, "We believe that health is natural and normal and will be our portion if we will but observe God's Natural Laws in our daily walk through this life!, (Galatians 6:7), We believe that God does not want us to be sick! The Bible tells us in III John 2 that God wishes 'above all things that thou mayest prosper and be in health, even as thy soul prospereth.' We believe that sickness comes ONLY when we violate the natural Laws God gave us to live by! **Disease is abnormal, unnatural and unnecessary!** The only exception to this statement would be sickness for the 'glory of God' or 'because of sin', (1 Corinthians 3:16-17). We believe that using treatments, drugs, radiation and surgical removal of body parts in an effort to bring about healing is unnatural to the body and interferes with healthful body functions and the body's efforts to heal itself!, (Mark 5:25-26). We reject the idea that sickness and disease are inevitable in our lives. Rather we contend that sickness and disease *will not occur unless there is sufficient cause!* Proverbs 26:2 says, '...the curse ***causeless*** *shall not come'*. We believe that no curse of sickness or ill health comes without a cause... and further, that if we will but ***eliminate the* CAUSE, *the curse (sickness) will usually go away and stay away!!!"***

For over 100 years, chiropractors have been talking about eliminating the cause of disease rather than the attempt to treat symptoms, which the medical profession has done for years. Pick up any magazine and look for the drug ads or watch any t. v. commercial. They will simply say take this medication and relieve the symptoms of headaches, of sinus problems, of digestive difficulties, of allergies, etc. Remove the symptoms, relieve the symptoms, or eliminate the symptoms. Get it? The thrust is always to handle the symptoms. The ads never say, "Let's not mask your symptoms and problems with drugs, let's try and get to the root of the problem once and for all! Just treating symptoms long enough can have disastrous results!

In 1899, D. D. Palmer wrote a piece entitled, "A Valuable Watch". I believe it speaks loudly and powerfully so I have reprinted it here in its entirety. Please read "A Valuable Watch":

"If you should let your watch fall or by any means get some parts of it displaced or injured so that it does not keep good time, or even refuses to run at all, you would take it to a watch doctor. Suppose that upon examination he should tell you that he would have to cut out one or two cogs or remove a wheel in order to make it run, would you leave it with him? No! Not even for one minute. 'I have carried that watch for many years, it has served me faithfully, it has always told me the correct time, and you cannot make me believe that the watch factory put in too many wheels or cogs'.

Why not use as good judgment in regards to your mother, wife, or daughter who are much more valuable? You would not let a jeweler cut out any portion of your watch. But how many, when mother, wife or daughter has had a fall or met with some injury, thereby displacing some portion of the anatomy so that she is unable to do as formerly, call in the family physician, whom they have learned to love and respect?

He makes a diagnosis and prescribes for her. Day after day he calls, takes the temperature, respiration, and feels the pulse and finds that her condition is no better. He finally advises you to take her to the repair shop, usually called a hospital. They there decide that an operation must be performed; some parts of her person must be removed, they have done all else they know and they must do something.

You would not trust your watch in the care of one whom your best reason told you would ruin it by the removal of some of its parts. But you will trust a person whom you love far more than the watch to the tender mercies of those who rifle women of their motherhood. You listen to the sophistry of the wise doctor; he is willing to take responsibility (as far as words go) and assures you that the operation of removing some parts of her body will put her on the road to recovery. You know that God did not put in any useless parts any more than the watch factory put in too many parts in your watch. With dread and fear you finally leave her, although you cannot help but think that the responsibility, the gain or loss, and the pay, all rest upon you and not the doctor.

You cease to use your reason. You not only leave your mother, wife, or daughter in the hands of the despoiler, but you also take your watch to the quack jeweler, who at once removes two cogs or a wheel and returns it to you, saying that he hopes it will now run all right. When you took your watch to the quack it did run, but it failed to correct time; now to your chagrin and disgust you find it will not run at all. You arrive at home and find that your mother, wife or daughter has been returned, pale, emaciated, and weak, but the physician assures you that all she now needs is time and rest. But you are doomed to disappointment for you find that time, like the doctor's knife, has not improved her condition, but on the contrary, she is now much more helpless than before you spent her time and your money.

You notify the jeweler of the condition of your watch. He tells you of his apprenticeship, of his experience in the business; that he can take the insides of a watch all out, and did so with yours, and found that it had too many wheels to run well, and that possibly there are too many in there yet; if you will let him have it once more he will call in some of his neighbors of like craft who are skilled in that line. They will hold council over it, examine it with a microscope and see for sure just what is the trouble, and so it comes to pass that you again leave your watch. Your family physician calls upon you and tells you he possibly did not cut enough of her insides, and advises you to return her to the shop. They will hold consultation and advise with the medical staff and know of a certainty just what and how much should be taken out. You again yield your better judgment to one whom you think ought to know better than you do and she is again taken from home and sympathizing friends.

In the meantime your watch is returned, or rather what is left of it. It no longer looks like the watch you once carried with so much pride, when everyone admired it and thought it such a beauty. The case is battered and full of wrinkles and bears no resemblance to its former self; it is ruined and destroyed beyond possibility of repair. Your mother, sister, or daughter as the case may be is again brought home, or, at least, what is left of her; but she bears no resemblance to the woman you once thought so plump and beautiful. She is no longer able to walk or take a step; she is only the shadow of her former figure. Her haggard, care-worn looks speaks only too plainly of her dreadful experience. The physician says the operation was a wonderful success. 'We have done all we can; give her the best of care while she lasts'".

We believe ourselves to be an ultra modern society

with advanced technology, capable of achieving wondrous things, and we are, in many aspects. But yet at the same moment in time, we are not very far removed from the world of 1899 when D. D. Palmer wrote, "The Valuable Watch". Today, we still see countless, needless surgeries, and removal of vital body parts. Mistakes are being perpetrated and healthy parts of the body are being surgically removed. Countless deadly drugs are administered that eventually destroy vital internal organs of the body forcing then, the removal of those devastated parts.

There may, in fact, be times when a drug needs to be administered or a surgery is absolutely necessary. It is not the life threatening or critical situations that I am writing about. It is the daily, casual use of drugs and surgery when nothing else less threatening or invasive has been tried and given an opportunity to work with the body's innate ability to heal. In a word, it comes down to laziness. People's laziness not to make the effort to seek alternatives and to seek choices. It is laziness to solely accept drugs as though they were just a piece of harmless apple pie you would eat with your milk. It is pure laziness not to truly accept the responsibility to care for and treasure this gift that God gave us—our bodies and our health.

Our bodies are temples.

"Do you not know that your body is the temple of the Holy Spirit who is in you, whom you have from God, and you are not your own? Therefore glorify God in your body and in your spirit, which are God's"..

-I Corinthians 6:19,20

If God were to speak to you today and personally hand you a gift, telling you it was from him with love, and that you should treasure it and care for it, how would you treat it? Would it be given the best of everything, the finest money could buy to care for it? Or would the gift be abused, misused, neglected, kicked around and treated as though it were a piece of scrap found discarded? Answer this to your heart and your God. Now look at how you treat the gift, the miracle of yourself!

God gives us the gift of life and of health. He provided everything we need to sustain us. No where in the Bible or any other spiritual or religious writings is it described that we are to use drugs or that we are to form harmful chemicals from the substances of the earth.

Isaiah had said, "Prepare a poultice of figs to apply it to the boil, and he will recover". There is no mention of cortisone injections, steroid creams, anti-inflammatories, acetaminophen, Prozac, Ritalin or any of the other thousands of drugs on the market. However, the Bible does say:

"Fruit trees of all kinds will grow on both banks of the river... their fruit will serve for food and their leaves for healing".

-Ezekiel 47:12

We are an intelligent species with the wisdom of the universe inside of us and the wisdom of the ages at our fingertips. When will we but listen and heed the call?

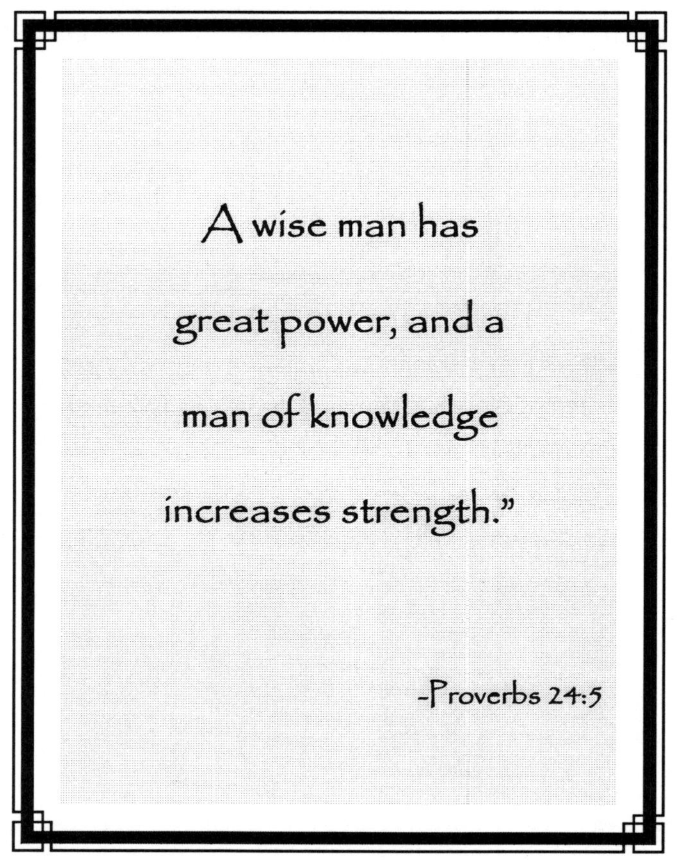
A wise man has
great power, and a
man of knowledge
increases strength."
-Proverbs 24:5

Chapter 12

The Harsh Reality God Wants You To Know

"My people are destroyed for lack of knowledge".
-Hosea 4:6

If you have not yet received the message in the reading so far, if the thoughts and quotes of great men haven't stirred you, if passages from the Scriptures haven't cemented the idea that the natural pathway to healing is the right way, the universal way, God's way. Then perhaps the hard facts on drugs in this next chapter will convince you. Just these mere statistics that follow on the effects that drugs have on the body; these alone if nothing else, may be the entire reason why God would want you to become an advocate for herbs and nutritional supplements. God's 101 reasons not to take drugs!

This chapter justifies the use of natural supplements and lets you know why it is not okay to go down the road of drugs. Ripped from the headlines, torn from the medical reports and journals, is further evidence to let us know that drugs are like a vicious wild animal that should not be taken lightly and definitely not let into our homes to play with our loved ones. The following are a synopsis of articles that deal with the problems of drugs. Read this, learn it, and share it with others. Do not let yourself be destroyed!

WARNING

Annual Deaths/U. S.		Ranking Cause of Death
Adverse Drug Reactions	Kills over 106,000 people	4th leading cause of death to properly prescribed medications
Stroke	Kills over 150,108 people	3rd leading cause of death
Cancer	Kills over 529,904 people	2nd leading cause of death
Heart Disease	Kills over 743,460 people	1st leading cause of death

*Note-These adverse drug reactions are to properly prescribed medications.

This does not take into account improperly prescribed medications or over-the-counter medications. The amount of people experiencing serious but non-fatal toxic reactions to properly prescribed medications was greater than 2 million!

Will you be counted amongst the dead or seriously ill?

W.W. J. D.?

Source: Journal of American Medical Association, April 15, 1998

Common Allergy Drug Interaction May Kill You!

(Prescription allergy medication hismanal, an antihistamine, mixed with grapefruit juice and other drugs like Prozac, may kill you). The F. D. A. reported a list of drugs that in combination could cause allergic deadly reactions or heart problems. Among the drugs listed were hypertension drugs, antibiotics, asthma drugs and more.

How many times a day does someone swallow medication with a harmless drink like grapefruit juice, never thinking that this simple action may just end their life? Should we have to live like this? I hope by now your answer is a resounding, No!

W. W. J. D.?

Source: "Interactions with RX Allergy Drug Pose Life Threatening Risk", D. A. Consumer, May-June 1998

Super Bacteria Threatens The World!

The (WHO) World Health Organization has issued numerous warnings and alerts stating that major epidemics such as "AIDS, Ebola and others may be linked to misuse and over use of antibiotics!" A 1996 report by the (WHO) said this about antibiotic use- "they are used by too many people to treat the wrong kind of infections at the wrong dosage and for the wrong period of time".

W.W.J.D.?

Source: "Vancomycin-resistant Enterococcus faecium colonization on children", Journal of Clinical Microbiology, Feb, 1999., World Health Report 1996, World Health Organization, Geneva, Switzerland, May 1996, Health Watch, Vol. 3, No. 12

IF YOU DON'T MIND THE RISK OF A STROKE, HEART ATTACK OR BLOOD CLOT...

Then there is a birth control pill that clears up your complexion!

Can you believe there is actually a television ad that promotes taking this certain birth control pill (orthtricycalene) because it also will clear up your skin? If you are taking a birth control pill you might as well kill two birds with one stone and take the one that also clears your skin! Oh, by the way, some minor side effects are **HEART ATTACK, STROKE, AND BLOOD CLOTS.** But hey, you will have clear skin!

First, women should not be on birth control pills. (They are very harmful to a woman's body). Secondly, if your skin is not clear yet, you are definitely too young!

W.W.J.D.?

Potential Birth Defects And Miscarriages from Cough Medicine

A two- year research project at the University of Nebraska Medical Center concluded that dextromethorphan, the key ingredient in cough and cold medicines may cause miscarriages and birth defects.

The research was done on chicken embryos, but the research team headed by Dr. Rosenquist notes that "modern molecular biology shows that the same genes regulate early development in virtually all species-from insects and worms to humans. Based on this, it can be predicted that the effects dextromethorphan had on the chicken embryos also would occur in human babies".

What happened? Chicken embryos were administered various doses of the drug over 3 days. Greater than half that were given the highest dose, died. Congenital defects like neural tube defects such as spina bifida, facial defects and cranial defects occurred in about one eighth of the survivors.

Dr. Rosenquist said several other things "a single dose is capable of causing a birth defect and that ultimately it could be the cause for a woman to have a miscarriage".

Another example of the potential hazards of what most people consider common harmless medications

W. W. J. D.?

Sources-Pediatric Research Jan 1998, pg. 1-7, "UNMC Study links use of Non-prescription Cough Medicine to Miscarriages, Birth defects", Media release, University of Nebraska, Jan.15, 1998, Health Watch Vol. 2, No. 11

HELLO, ANTIBIOTICS DON'T WORK ON COLDS! TREATING COMMON COLDS WITH ANTIBIOTICS ARE COMPLETELY INEFFECTIVE (USELESS)

Most colds are caused by viruses. Not bacteria! Antibiotics are completely ineffective against viruses. Stuart Levy, president of American Society for Microbiology stated, "Almost all cases of the common cold are caused by viruses, and antibiotics do not work on viral infections". Yet doctors, continue to prescribe antibiotics. It is estimated 60 percent of all colds are treated with antibiotics costing some $37.5 million per year in the U.S. When will it stop? When you become aware, take responsibility for your own health and say no more!

W. W. J. D.?

Source: Journal of Chemical Microbiology, February 4, 1998; 36: 539-542., Health Watch, Volume 2, Number 12.

Sleeping pills are hazardous to your health, similar to smoking 1 to 2 packs of cigarettes per day.

Research at UCSD found that ingesting sleeping pills at least 30 times per month was similar to the hazardous affects of smoking 1 to 2 packs of cigarettes per day.

The reason that those people who use prescription sleeping pills on a daily basis are nearly 30 percent more likely to die within a 6 year follow up period than those that don't.

W.W.J.D.?

Sources: "Sleeping Pills", Media Advisory, University of California, San Diego June 3, 1998, Health Watch, Vol. 3, No. 5

Soy May Just Save Your Life!

Over 50 studies seem to indicate that 25 grams of soy protein in a diet low in cholesterol and saturated fat may reduce the risk of heart disease.

Heart disease is the #1 killer of Americans. "Soy protein with naturally occurring isoflavons can lower blood cholesterol levels 7 to 10 percent, which translates into a 14 to 20 percent reduction in heart disease risk".

What do you think is better, a little soy or dangerous drugs?

W.W.J.D.?

Source: F. D. A. Publishers, Proposed Rule on Soy Heart-Health Claim, Protein Technologies International, Nov 13, 1998, Health Watch Volume 3, No. 8

Dozens of Children Die, Others Need Liver Transplants Due to Over-the-counter Medication

A report in the Journal of Pediatrics stated that slightly higher dosages of acetaminophen have killed more than two dozen U.S. children, three more required liver transplants! Liver toxicity was documented in 55 children, this due to acetaminophen, which is the active ingredient in Tylenol and Excedrin. It is the most common over-the-counter pain medication. Researchers warn parents about the dangers of exceeding the recommended dosages.

According to Dr. James Heubi, the lead researcher, he feels that "this probably only represents a fraction of the total number of cases that have had this problem in this country".

W.W.J.D.?

Source-Journal of Pediatrics, January, 1998, Health Watch, Volume 2, No. 11

$400 Million + Cost to New York City to Treat Staph Infections!

Staphylococcus Aureus, the leading cause of bacterial infections is becoming drug resistant. New York City spent over 400 million dollars to treat 13,500 people. "The infections doubled the average length of hospital stays to 20 days, increased per patient costs to $32,100 and the death rate to 10 percent, as compared to average hospital stays of nine days, costing $13,263, with mortality rates of 4.1 percent". This, according to Robert J. Rubin, M. D. director of the study.

He also said that staph bacteria are the lead cause of pneumonia in hospitals. What is very alarming is the fact that 95 percent of staph infections don't respond to penicillin or ampicillin, and 30 percent of all infections don't respond to second-line antibiotics.

I would advise not spending any time in a hospital!

W.W.J.D.?

Source-Emerging Infectious Diseases, Jan-March, 1999, Volume 5, No. 1, Health Watch Volume 3, No. 12

Stroke Risk Increased By Daily Aspirin Intake!

This would alarm me. Does it alarm you?

Daily aspirin intake was shown by research to lower the risk for heart attacks. However, it greatly increased the risk for hemorrhagic stroke by 84 percent!

I do not think this is an acceptable risk, do you? In fact, in 1988 the researchers warned that patients should not—that is, should not take aspirin to prevent heart disease!

However, aspirin manufacturers continue to flood the media and advertise the benefits of lowering the risk of heart attack, even though the major side effect is STROKE!

Aspirin is not a safe drug.

Allergic reactions to aspirin kill 1600 children per year. Aspirin makes patients with arterial blockage to the brain 3 times more likely to have a stroke. 300 milligrams of aspirin a day cause gastrointestinal hemorrhages in 31 percent of patients. Other side effects—bleeding ulcers, confusion, dizziness, anemia and more! Why take aspirin?

W.W.J.D.?

Source: Health Watch, Volume 3, No. 9

Suicide Linked to High Blood Pressure Drug!

Calcium channel blockers are used to treat high blood pressure. A research team found that those people who used calcium channel blockers were five times more likely to commit suicide than those people not taking the drug. The study was done on 152 Swedish cities of 7.3 million people.

W. W. J. D.?

Source: British Medical Journal, No. 1733, Volume 316, March 7, 1998, Health Watch, Volume 3, No. 1

Eat Tums—
Get all the calcium you need!

I don't think so, but you've got to love those commercials that try and sell you that idea. And of course, some people do buy it!

In fact, a Mayo Clinic study revealed that 1,600 milligrams of calcium a day given to women gave about a one percent increase in bone density!

The Mayo Clinic studied 177 women for four years. These women were aged 61 to 70 and had no history of osteoporosis. To get 1600 mg. of calcium, a person would have to ingest approximately six extra strength Tums daily! That is a considerable amount and can have severe consequences.

If you read the Tums package, it reads, "Do not take more than ten tablets in a 24 hour period or use the maximum dosage of this product for more than two weeks…"

So why do they advertise a calcium benefit?

W. W. J. D.?

Sources: Media Advisory, Mayo Clinics, March 27, 1998, Journal of Bone and Mineral Research, Health Watch, Volume 3, No. 1, February, 1998

Risk for Esophageal Cancer Increased by Radiation Therapy

It seems that while treating women with radiation for breast cancer, their long- term risk for esophageal cancer increases!

Columbia-Presbyterian Medical Center did the research. They reviewed the records of over 220,000 breast cancer patients from 1973 to 1993. These included irradiated patients and those that were not. What they found was that patients who had received radiation therapy were approximately four to five times more likely to develop cancer of the esophagus than those who had not been treated with radiation or women in society.

In a previous study, they found that radiation treatment for breast cancer increased the risk for lung cancer, but was significantly higher for those who smoked. In fact, these smokers who had been irradiated were at 40 times the risk. Although not sure yet, the researchers suspect that there may be an even greater risk with esophageal cancer, radiation and smoking!

It is currently estimated that one out of every 2,000 women with breast cancer develops esophageal cancer.

W. W. J. D.?

Source: "Radiation Treatment for Breast Cancer Raises Risk for Esophageal", Columbia-Presbyterian Medical Center media release January 22, 1998 Health Watch, Volume 2, No. 11

Could your cardiologist be taking antioxidants but advising you differently?

The answer is an emphatic—yes!

In a survey reported in the American Journal of Cardiology, some cardiologists, 44%, actually take antioxidant supplements! These include Vitamin C, Vitamin E, and beta-carotene.

There is a ponderous amount of evidence that shows antioxidants can help prevent cancer and coronary artery disease, yet this same survey revealed that only 37% of cardiologists are recommending this preventive course to their patients! Remember earlier in the book, I talked about the hazards of taking aspirin therapy to reduce the risk of heart attack? Well, this same survey revealed that even fewer doctors take the same aspirin therapy recommended to patients!

Remember—

W.W. J. D.?

Source: American Journal of Cardiology, 1997, Health Watch, Volume 2, Number 7

The elderly are at high risk due to dangerous drug prescriptions.

The American Journal of Health System Pharmacy published a survey showing that one in twenty prescriptions given to seniors included a dangerous drug they shouldn't have.

"Because of age-related changes in the structure and function of various organs, certain drugs may cause serious— sometimes life-threatening side effects in the elderly. Inappropriate prescriptions most often include the drugs diazepam, propoxyphene, dipyridamole, amitriptyline, and chlordiazepoxide, commonly known by the brand names Valium, Darvon, Persantine, Elavil, and Librium.

According to researchers, the odds of receiving a prescription for a potentially inappropriate medication are greater when elderly patients receive any of the following:

- Prescriptions for more than one medication;
- Care from a physician to whom they were referred;
- Prescriptions for dipyridamole or an antispasmodic agent such as cyclobenzaprine, or Flexeril (which have little benefit in the elderly); or
- Care at an outpatient department not in a metropolitan area.

Information about the outpatient visits came from the 1997 National Hospital Ambulatory Medical Care Survey, conducted by the National Center for Health Statistics.

Serious life threatening side effects scare me. Does it scare you? Often times elderly take medications with blind faith that the "doctor knows what's best", or because they aren't given any options. I wonder how many people would take a drug if they were told it could end their life?

W.W.J.D.?

Source: American Journal of Health-System Pharmacy, March 11, 1999, Health Watch, Volume 3, No. 12

Medications (drugs) are not to be trifled with, nor should they be dismissed as non-threatening substances to be so casually and freely used as they are today. It is crucial to one's life to be educated about the risks, and dangers of medications. The taking of even one pill can have devastating effects. The illusion that drugs are harmless substances and can only do good can kill you!

Iron Eyes Cody, the famous Native American makes the point another way in his story, "The Snake":

Many years ago, Indian youths would go away in solitude to prepare for manhood. One such youth hiked into a beautiful valley, green with trees, bright with flowers. There he fasted. But on the third day, as he looked up at the surrounding mountains, he noticed one tall rugged peak, capped with dazzling snow. "I will test myself against that mountain," he thought. He put on his buffalo-hide shirt, threw his blanket over his shoulders and set off to climb the peak. When he reached the top he stood on the rim of the world. He could see forever, and his heart swelled with pride. Then he heard a rustle at his feet, and looking down, he saw a snake. Before he could move, the snake spoke:

"I am about to die," said the snake. "It is too cold for me up here and I am freezing. There is no food and I am starving. Put me under your shirt and take me down to the valley." "No," said the youth. "I am forewarned. I know your kind. You are a rattlesnake. If I pick you up you will bite, and your bite will kill me."

"Not so," said the snake. "I will treat you differently. If you do this for me, you will be special. I will not harm you."

The youth resisted awhile, but this was a very persuasive snake with a beautiful marking. At last the youth tucked it under his shirt and carried it down to the valley. There he laid it gently on the grass, when suddenly the snake coiled, rattled and leapt, biting him on the leg.

"But you promised--" cried the youth. "You knew what I was when you picked me up," said the snake as it slithered away.

And now, wherever I go, I tell that story. I tell it especially to the young people of this nation who might be tempted by drugs. I want them to remember the words of the snake:

YOU KNEW WHAT I WAS
WHEN YOU PICKED ME UP.

WHAT WOULD JESUS
DO?
WOULD HE PICK UP THE
SNAKE?

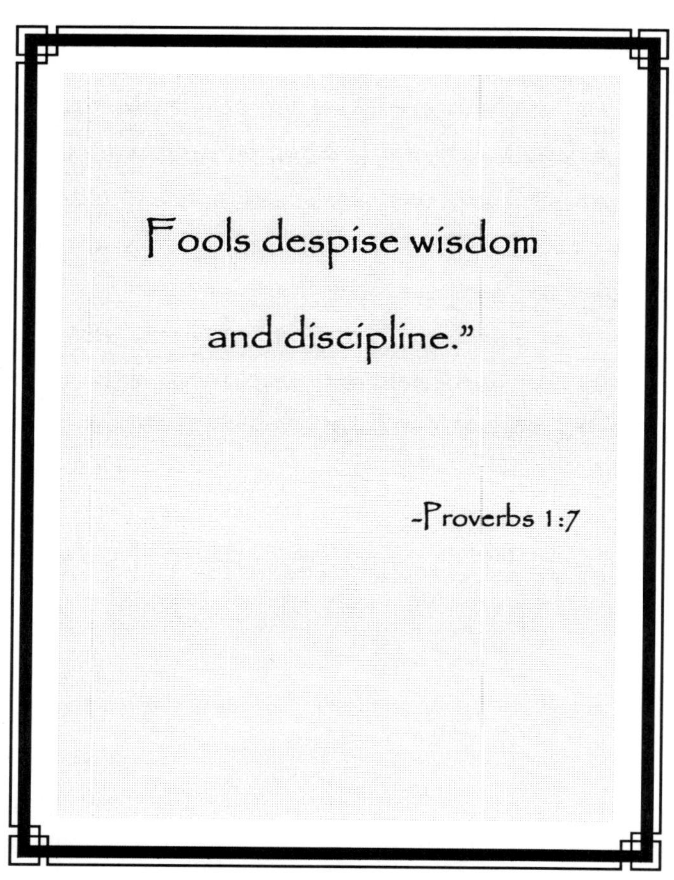

Fools despise wisdom

and discipline."

-Proverbs 1:7

Chapter 13

The Dangers of Listening To The Wrong People

As a chiropractor, I have a natural preponderance for natural healing. Allowing the body's innate intelligence to work freely. In my earlier book, **"Dare to Break Through the Pain,** ***A Guide to Eliminating Back & Neck Pain Naturally Without Drugs or Surgery!"*** I speak to the issue of drugs. Not just street drugs, but prescription and non-prescription drugs called medicines or medications. The following is a short excerpt from that book:

"I want you to think about the powerful and conflicting messages that society is sending to the children of this country about drugs. They are constantly told that drugs on the street are bad for them. They are told to 'just say no'".

Yet they see, and are around drugs all day. Their young minds cannot really make the distinction between the mind-altering drugs of the street and the feel good over-the-counter or prescription drugs. The messages these kids receive from the earliest days are by good intentioned, loving people—their parents and their doctors. Then by some of the most powerful, life altering, influencing entities in the world—ADVERTISING! The messages all these people are sending is that drugs—the right drugs—are OK!

Advertising bombards their conscious and subconscious minds with the idea that it is okay to take drugs to feel better. Sometimes you do not even need your doctor's prescription, because you can get the drugs over-the-counter at a DRUG store. But, if those do not work you can go to the doctor and get more potent and powerful drugs. The same thing happens on the street.

First there is experimentation to see the effects of the drug. It is enjoyable so they continue on. They become addicted. The drug is not giving them the same high so now they have to seek out a more powerful stimulus. And so it goes.

The children see this, they copy the adults and then they too become adults and their whole lives revolve around the medicine cabinet.

They have been groomed by the drug companies to rely on the drugs for everything. Every little ache and pain—take a pill for it. If your head hurts—take a pill for it. If you ate too much—take a pill for it. Now there are advertisements that suggest taking a pill before you even have a symptom. Take this pill before you eat so that you do not have the pain or indigestion. If you plan to eat something that you know will disagree with you, it is okay! Take a pill before you eat it.

If you become obese, you better take that pill to lose weight. If you have had a rough day—take a pill to calm down.

If you cannot sleep at night—take a pill.

If you are under too much stress—take a pill.

Or better yet have a smoke and a drink—then take a pill.

And, of course, if you do not want a baby—that is right—take a pill!

We are a doomed society, with tattered lives and obviously our salvation must come from the medications, pills, potions, lotion, and solutions. Or so the pharmaceutical companies would like us to believe. Does anyone else think this sounds like madness?! In this country we always think that big is better. If one pill works then ten should work ten times as good.

Why can't we be more like the Germans? U. S. A. Today reported that "Over the past 50 years, the number of Germans who have lived to be 100 years of age and beyond has increased more than 2,000 percent! This is because Germans demand herbal medicines which have fewer side effects or harmful interactions than prescription drugs".

More and more coverage is being given to alternative medicine. In fact, because it is threatening to the standard medical model of sickness care, the medical system is doing research into the phenomenon. The most recent study from Harvard Medical School showed that Americans are now turning more towards alternative medicine practitioners like chiropractors and naturopaths than their primary care physician. They show that visits to alternative health practitioners is up 47 percent since 1990. However, as I mentioned earlier in the book, there are only 55,000 licensed chiropractors in the U.S. and only 1,500 licensed naturopaths—yet there are 849,000 medical doctors. We need your help!

It is about time Americans stop listening to the A. M. A. and the pharmaceutical companies and wake up to what the rest of the world already knows.

Are you ready to have a positive impact on the health of the planet?

Can you accept that you are capable of changing the world!?

Right now our planet is in a critical state. Yes, we still have wars, prejudice, homelessness and more. But I am talking about the continual insidious drugging of the planet. The planned systematic attempts at drugging each and every individual to totally dominate and control us. Through drugs, enslave us and bring us to financial ruin, creating future generations of drug addicts to legally prescribed drugs and all the while making pharmaceutical companies billions of dollars. It is occurring illegally in the streets, but it is happening legally on every corner of this country and ultimately the world. They will not stop until complete and ultimate domination is achieved. They will have us all working to support our legally prescribed drugs because drugs prices will continue to skyrocket. If everyone in the family is on drugs, how will a family afford it? This may sound crazy to you, but just think about it. We don't have to be dominated, we don't have to be placed under financial duress, and we don't have to be victimized. We have choices.

"All suffering is caused by an obstacle in the path of a force. See that you are not your own obstacle".

-Elbert Hubbard

I hope I am getting your attention. There is a war on! If you are not yet aware, pharmaceutical companies and certain medical groups are doing everything in their power to eliminate and eradicate alternative medicine. And if they can't eliminate it they want to control it. Quite simply, alternative health care is cutting into their pie and they are losing more money and power over you! Even though billions of dollars are made on drugs, the pharmaceutical companies are just like an addict—they continue to want more and more until they have it all. It continually becomes harder for them to get their "fix".

They aren't satisfied with 10 billion, they need 25 billion, 50 billion, 145 billion dollars and on and on. If you are reading this book, you have a distinct interest in what will occur, whether financially or physically. The war is about trying to take away your freedoms. Your ability to choose the kind of health care provider you want. To take away your ability to buy or sell nutritional products. All of this, in the guise of trying to protect you because you aren't intelligent or educated enough to know what is good or bad for you. But they do—

"A father without a father has difficulty balancing. A master without a master is dangerous".

-365 Tao

The pharmaceutical companies seem to have no master.

From Ecclesiastes— "A time for everything, there is a time for everything and a season for every activity under Heaven: A time to plant and a time to uproot-a time to tear down and a time to build. A time to be silent and a time to speak". IT'S TIME! I believe it is time to tear down the pharmaceutical companies drug hold over the country and the world. Time to uproot the omnipotent idea that drugs are the cure all and answer to every physical, chemical and mental challenge that faces a human being. Time to plant the seeds of a new renaissance of healing. A time to speak our minds and our hearts, take responsibility for our health and not allow others to dictate what methods of healing are best for us based on the propaganda that is spewed out. The drug propaganda machine is huge very powerful and has vast resources. Their advertising gives people a false sense of reality. It lures people into believing that everyone should take drugs for every purpose and not fear the consequences. Drugs are portrayed as man's best friend!

Every individual must be ready to fight to keep our rights. We have to be ready to fax, write letters, call our congressman and legislators to let them know we want control, we want to be able to choose. What do I mean? Well, the American Medical Association (A. M. A.) had a plan for 1999 as part of its legislative priority to work with congress to place vitamins, dietary supplements and herbal remedies under federal regulation! What they want is to require all supplements and herbal remedies to undergo the F. D. A. approval process for safety and efficacy. This is one step closer to full control at which point you will only be able to purchase certain vitamins, minerals and herbal supplements with a doctor's prescription. The saddest part of that is that medical doctors have no idea about nutrition. In fact, they have less than two hours of nutrition classroom teaching in medical school. Do we really want them in charge?

It's time to listen to what our innate intelligence is trying to tell us. The message is continually being delivered. All too often we do not open the door to accept it.

It is interesting that the medical profession has self-proclaimed their profession to be the saviors and healers, the watch keepers of all of mankind's health and illnesses. Partially because they believe no one is as capable as they are and secondly they enjoy the power and money. They are unwilling to share any of this with other disciplines of healing. Even more interesting is that they never look at their own mistakes or odd ideas of healing, but focus their attention on others as if they were quacks. For example, did you know that physicians who were trying to rid him of his sore throat bled George Washington to death? Yes, the father of our country, the man who led the Revolutionary Army to victory, survived battles, hardships of war, bitter winter battle campaigns, died in his bed from being bled to cure his sore throat.

The medical profession has gone from embracing chiropractic, herbs, osteopathy, homeopathy, Chinese medicine, and using and prescribing herbs to condemning all of the above. Now once again, they are starting to embrace some of these same healing disciplines. Why?-money and power. At some point in time, the pharmaceutical companies got hold of the medical profession, convinced them natural remedies didn't work, took too much time and serious money couldn't be made by using them. So synthetic drugs were the way to go.

I am in possession of a book that belongs to my mother and has been in the family for years. This book is entitled, "Library of Health, Complete Guide to Prevention & Cure of Disease", copyrighted in 1916. It is a book designed for lay people to use at home to heal themselves. This book was written by medical doctors from all over the world, such places as Vienna, Cuba, Canada, Mexico, Buenos Aires, London, New York, Philadelphia and even a doctor of chiropractic from Davenport, Iowa. Not only does this medical book have a section on chiropractic, but the table of contents lists the following: "Foods and their

Digestion", "Homeopathy", "Osteopathy", "Chiropractic", "Hydrotherapy", "Massage", "Eclectic Medicine" "The Japanese Method", "The German Home Treatment", "Mental Healing", Including "Mesmerism", "Hypnotism", "Mind Cure", "Christian Science", "Telepathy", "Palmistry", "Physical Culture & Body Building", "The Science of Breath and a Series of Remedial Exercises", and even a section on "Jiu Jitsu". In part II of the book are "Treats of the Organic (vegetable) Materials used in Medicine. Superb Colored Illustrations of Eighty-four Plants, Fruits, and Vegetables". This is quite an impressive collection of natural healing remedies from a profession that seems to invalidate all other healing modalities.

This book is so complete that it gives weights and measures, exact recipes to create the medicines, adult v. s. child doses. It is obviously a book written by people who truly cared for their fellow man and were interested in their health and healing. Prevention of disease was a tool to empower common men and women to care for themselves. There is no hint of political agendas. It is a book for the people. I compliment the dedicated doctors and writers for putting together such a wonderful creation for man during that time period.

These words from the creators of the book: "This knowledge aims to teach prevention rather than cure. It is a well-known fact that over fifty percent of the sickness that comes to the home is unnecessary and preventable if the people have the proper knowledge. The right kind of information in the hands of the mother will prevent unnecessary sickness, take care of accidents and emergencies, and save thousands of lives".

The authors obviously felt that chiropractic, herbal remedies, homeopathy, Japanese medicine, German remedies, and more were of significant importance to the health and well being of the human body. Additionally, that people had a right and responsibility to learn as much as they could to care for themselves and their families. This is a far cry from the thoughts and feelings of many of today's doctors, and certainly the pharmaceutical companies. Western medicine has become arrogant to the point that it dismisses ideas, concepts and philosophies that are outside the medical community or outside of the U. S. and therefore, outside of their control. The U. S. thinks it isn't even worthy of thought. We are a nation that has become too arrogant and self-righteous and prideful. We invalidate and ignore reason, good thought, proven methods whether scientific or clinical. It is time to embrace the universal intelligence once again and let go of some of that control. Trust our inner beings and have faith in God, our creator, who knows how to care for us, and has given us the means to participate in our health and well being.

"For wisdom will enter your heart. And knowledge will be pleasant to your soul. Discretion will protect you, and understanding will guide you".

-Proverbs 2:10-11

"Satan himself masquerades as an angel of light. It is not surprising, then, if his Servants masquerade as Servants of righteousness. Their end will be what their actions deserve."

-II Corinthians 14:15

Chapter 14

A Time to Choose

"Back to the Garden" is a newsletter produced by Reverend George Malkmus. As I read through one of the issues, I became very interested to find that Reverend Malkmus held many of the same views as myself, and most of my colleagues as well as many others in what has become dubbed as alternative medicine, (I prefer natural healing). He speaks against medicines. Since this was my first exposure to his writings, I was intrigued and decided to order all of his back issues. I was very pleased to come upon an article in the Winter/Spring 1996 issue entitled, "Drugs: A Killer of Mankind".

It was refreshing to see a man of faith, a Reverend, not a natural healing practitioner, speaking out against drugs! Not just street or illegal drugs, but commonly prescribed medications and legal over-the-counter medications. He echoes and voices what many say, teach and lecture about—drugs are poisons! They are toxins that do not belong in the human body. There was one particular piece of information that I was unaware of and pleased to learn, so I thought I would share it with you. I'm sure Reverend Malkmus won't mind.

I quote him completely: "In the Bible, in the book of Revelation chapter 18 and verse 23, we are told, 'For by thy sorceries (drugs) were all nations deceived'. The biblical word for sorceries comes from the Greek word, Phar-ma-kia, when in today's language would be translated as drugs." That is so powerful I just need to write it again—sorceries comes from the Greek, Phar-ma-kia, translates as drugs. And in the Bible it says, "...for by thy sorceries were all nations deceived". Does this not require some thought? Is this not of truly biblical significance for our time? We see it happening all around us.

Remember that I mentioned the planet is being drugged? Prozac is being produced for dogs and also used on children. Over 1.5 million kids between the ages of 6 to 10 are on anti-depressants. Children are being prescribed Ritalin in record numbers, and it has been estimated that 4.4 million children have been labeled with A.D.H.D. in North America. There are some schools where Ritalin is given out in the morning and again at lunch, and 50 percent of the children are on the drug. Ninety percent of the Ritalin use is right here in the United States. What message is in that statistic? In September of 1997, it was reported that sales of Ritalin were approaching $400 million annually! This is only one drug. Others being used are Dexidrine, Adderall, Cylert, Syban, Luvox and Zoloft. I wonder how many kids are in the world today? Get my point?

Well, a group called C.H.A.D.D. does. (Children and adults with attention deficit disorder). They attack natural healing methods for A.D.D. and lobby to make Ritalin non-prescription! Guess who partially funds C.H.A.D.D.? Ciba-Geigy, the very pharmaceutical company that makes Ritalin! How many children are in the world? Don't be surprised if we start seeing more suicides, mom and pop killers, and serial murderers!

Did you know the Wall Street Journal reported that Ciba-Geigy supplies schools with informational material about A.D.D.? And that "the United Nations International Control Board advised the U.S. Drug Enforcement Administration that this could be seen as hidden advertising of a controlled substance and may be in violation of international laws"? Did you know that Ritalin and cocaine act basically the same way in the brain? And that cocaine addicts cannot tell the difference between cocaine and Ritalin when the drugs are administered to them? Did you know that Ritalin is a Class II controlled substance? So is morphine, and cocaine.

Is it possible to believe that drugs could just be the downfall of our country and of the world? Isn't this reason enough to stop looking for the easy way out, reaching for that "cure all" medicine? Isn't this reason enough to look towards natural alternative healing methods? To eat properly and supplement with herbs and vitamins/minerals? To truly embrace this as a way of healing, of health, and of disease control. Do we actually need a medicine (drug) cabinet? Can't we replace it with an herbal cabinet? Should each one of us make it a mission in life to heal ourselves, our families, and share natural healing with others? Absolutely!! Our survival truly depends on it. Don't be fooled. The drug companies know that herbs are encroaching on their turf. They don't like it. They mean to stop it either by totally eliminating it, or controlling it. This is why you are now seeing major pharmaceutical companies producing herbal remedies.

When the only choice for healing you are given is drugs, then your choice will be drugs.

But when you are given the opportunity to evaluate multiple forms of healing and research and understand all their possibilities, shortcomings, or side effects, now you can make a more rational and well informed decision.

"For we wrestle not against flesh and blood but against principalities, against powers, against rulers of the darkness of this world, against spiritual wickedness in high places".

-Ephesians 6:12

It is not easy to go against tradition and the tradition in this country and in so many industrialized countries is to use medication and surgery as answers to all health problems.

There is a great sense of satisfaction from knowing the truth. Almost as though you have the inside secrets and yet everyone else is laughing at you or condemning you. You know in your heart and soul that the truth will one day be shown and your dedication to it will be vindicated. History is riddled with people, who for one reason or another, chose not to follow the pack, but to lead. They had the courage to venture out with new ideas, new inventions, and new philosophies that perhaps didn't fit the status quo and made people uneasy or uncomfortable. They have been persecuted, martyred, executed, ridiculed, and thought to be charlatans, quacks, devils.

People like Joan of Arc, a woman who fought for God and was burned at the stake. Christopher Columbus held the unpopular belief that the world was not flat, but round. Thomas Moore, Leonardo DaVince, Gallileo, and others looked to the stars. The Roman Empire persecuted Christians who held true to their faith. They were tortured, thrown to the lions and put to death because of their beliefs.

Countless people throughout time have suffered at the hands of others when they dared to dream a brand new dream, challenging people's awareness or comfort zones. When people are asked to think and change, they become resistant. Chiropractors know this all too well.

Since the inception of chiropractic healing, the medical establishment has tried to invalidate and erase chiropractic. In fact, the persecution was so real that they falsely accused chiropractors of practicing medicine without a license, and successfully had chiropractors imprisoned. Although many would have you believe this is ancient history, the last two chiropractors jailed was as recent as 1975 in the state of Louisiana! People have been fined and their businesses raided and shut down for selling nutritional products that claim to have healing properties. People, like electricity will follow the path of least resistance. Future generations always look back and wonder how could people not have seen the answers that seem to be so plainly in front of them. How could they be that ignorant? If we do the right things now, future generations will reflect back to this period of our history and wonder how we could have been so ignorant, so gullible. And how close we came to annihilating ourselves because of drugs. If, we do things right. If we don't there will be no one sane left to look back, except those few in control.

Claim your Spiritual Destiny—Own your responsibility to Mankind

God has given us the fundamental guide—the Bible. It tells us to seek natural healing. To use everything on this planet to sustain us, to follow His words, and share our gifts with others.

No where in the Bible, in Ayurvedic writings, in the writing of Koran, or other great books, are we directed to live a life controlled by chemical substances created by man. Solely manipulated by greedy individuals for the sole purpose of reaping riches upon themselves and keeping the masses subservient and addicted.

Who do you think will be in the favor of God when we are all seated before Him on judgment day? The person or company that pushes drugs in the world or the person or company that educates, enlightens and attempts to heal the world through natural means?

"It is easier for a camel to go through the eye of a needle than for a rich man to enter the kingdom of God".

-Matthew 19:24

What is your purpose on this planet? Why are you here? What is the meaning of your life? Will anyone care when you are gone? Who will have benefited by your existence and your life?

"Lives of great men all remind us,

We can make our lives sublime,

And departing leave behind us

Footprints on the sands of time".

-Longfellow

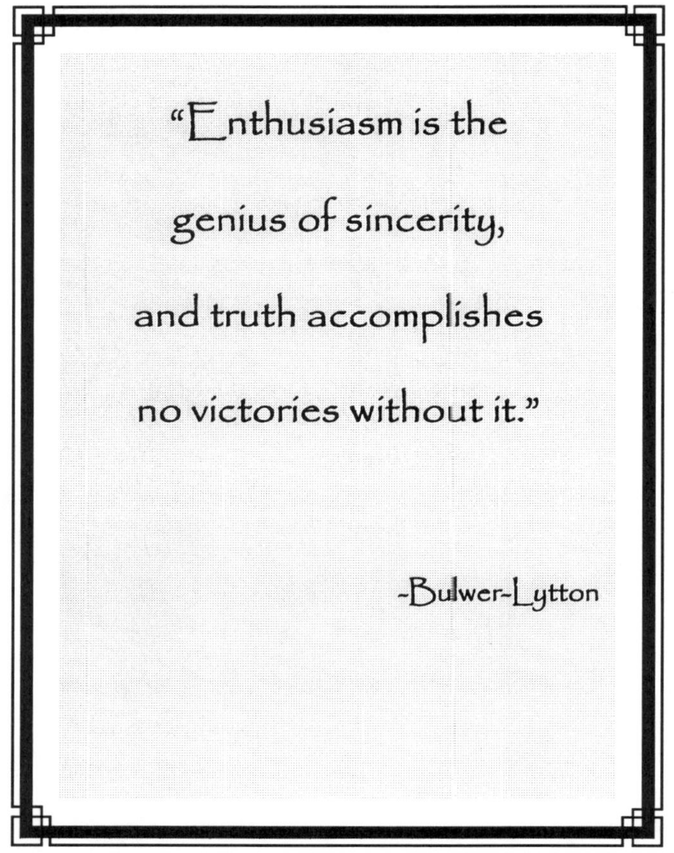

"Enthusiasm is the
genius of sincerity,
and truth accomplishes
no victories without it."
-Bulwer-Lytton

Chapter 15

Leaving Your Footprints in the Sand

Multitudes of self-help guides' men, marketing gurus, salesmen of salesmen will speak to and write books about enthusiasm! It is the one ingredient needed to sell anything to anyone or get someone to buy. It doesn't matter if you are an experienced professional salesman or if you are trying to get a date, or sell dad on why you need to borrow the car! It is enthusiasm that will make or break the deal.

Winston Marsh, one of the leading marketers and lecturers in Australia talks about the boomerang theory—"Remember that boomerangs were used in Australia by the indigenous people to hunt kangaroo. Upon throwing the boomerang, if the boomerang hits the target, both the kangaroo and boomerang drop. But if the target is missed, the boomerang comes back to the thrower. The boomerang theory says that 'whatever you throw out comes back to you'. If you give out enthusiasm you will get it back, if you give out honesty you will get it back. He believes the most important ingredient in business success is sheer unmitigated enthusiasm".

I have to definitely agree. If you have faith, confidence and belief in your product, services and ideas and you apply enthusiasm to this, well, then there is unlimited potential for health, healing, and success! If you are enthusiastic about your God, you are unstoppable. If your are enthusiastic about the herbs you take and sell—there will be nothing short of miraculous healing.

How much do you believe in your product and can you radiate your enthusiasm to the other person in such a way that it is contagious? So that, they have to have it and they want to buy whatever you are selling because of the enthusiasm you radiated. Well, enthusiasm is a substance that is critical to sales, but even more so to life itself. Without enthusiasm, life can become routine, mundane, boring and eventually it can become negative and depressing. Soon your whole outlook is affected. Your mind and state of consciousness is affected until your total health is negatively impacted. Your mind, body and spirit are laid wide open and susceptible for every disease that wants to come along and take up residence in your body. Enthusiasm is linked to laughter. When we are enthusiastic we laugh, we are happy, positive, motivated. Every cell in our bodies can feel the joy and express the life force that is magnified. For years, Reader's Digest has had a section of jokes and cute little stories that are designed to bring us laughter and lighten our load. It is called, "Laughter is the Best Medicine". This is true!

But you know who knew this before we even did? Do you know who designed us with this fantastic, self-healing mechanism already installed, ready to go? Of course, God—our Supreme Being—the essence of our souls, the light of our lights. It was not by accident, it was by design that we were given enthusiasm. We just have to learn to tap into it properly to heal. My good friend, Paul Turnbull in his book, "The Graduate and the Master", explains enthusiasm this way. "You see, enthusiasm comes from the Greek meaning 'possessed by a God, inspired'. EN; in + THEOS, God. This means a flow of emotion, known as enthusiasm is poured into the body from a spiritual source, to inspirit."

So you see, enthusiasm is a very important ingredient in health. A special gift, directly from God. Enthusiasm can help one heal. It can help one to understand why herbs and nutritional supplements are so important. Enthusiasm can be transferred from one human being to another without so much as a touch. Because it happens on an innate level; an electrical charge being passed from one human to another. It can happen one on one or in groups.

If you have ever been to a M.L.M. meeting on nutritional healing products, you know what I mean. If you haven't, I urge you to go. The enthusiasm these people have for their products is contagious. It is powerful. You can feel the electricity and the potential power for healing—mind, body, and soul!

"A happy heart makes the face cheerful, but heartache crushes the spirit".

-Proverbs 15:13

Dr. Norman Vincent Peale said, "those persons who consistently live with joy and enthusiasm seem to achieve a remarkable mastery over circumstances". Is it possible to overcome sickness and disease? Can we become the masters over our circumstances? Yes, we can. However, we will never accomplish this if our bodies, minds and souls are under the devastating control of drugs! We must make use of the natural healing methods that God provided for us so that we truly elevate ourselves to a state of ultimate health, free from sickness and disease and then we will be able to enjoy our full human potential of excellence.

Pray about your success. Pray for healing. Pray for knowledge of what you speak and what you seek.

You'll Never Walk Alone

I said, "The path is steep."
He said, "I'm at your side."
I said, "But I am weak."
He said, "For you I died."

I said, "Dark valleys come."
He said, "I'll guide you through."
I said, "But I'm not brave."
He said, "I'll walk with you."

I said, "Be Light to me,
And Strength as I go on."
He said, "I'm more. I'm Love.
You'll never walk alone."
You Can Make It

-Perry Tanksley

"My Son, do not forget
my teaching, but keep
my commands in
your heart for they will
prolong your life many
years and bring
you prosperity."

-Proverbs 3:1-2

Chapter 16

Healing the Planet

Earlier in the book, I quoted from Reverend Malkmus' newsletter concerning drugs.

"For by thy sorceries were all nations deceived".

-Revelations 18:23

I have shown biblical references that speak to the fact that we are our brothers keepers and that the health of the planet depends on us all.

Many biblical scholars, lay people, educators and others are suggesting that the world is in a very dangerous and critical point. That this is the end of times. Whether this is true or not, whether you believe or not, even the person of little faith, and little education can look at the violent times in this country and the devastation and tragedies in the world today and know deep in their hearts that evil exists. Darkness is over shadowing light, the world is in chaos and positive loving and healing actions have to be taken to elevate human beings back to a place of health, respect, and honor.

I have been suggesting that medications and drugs create much of the ill health and pain in the world today. Reverend Malkmus quoted that "For by thy sorceries were all nations deceived".

Many Catholics and non-Catholics believe that the

Mother of God, the Blessed Virgin Mary has been visiting our world through apparitions to warn us of our lack of love for each other and petition us to change. She has been seen by millions throughout the world for centuries, but is currently appearing even more frequently as never before.

Whether you believe the Virgin Mary is the mother of God or whether she is appearing to others on this earth, the message that is being delivered in her name is incredibly powerful, and bears repeating.

In the book, "For the Soul of the Family", Thomas Petrisko interviewed Estela Ruiz who has purported to have apparitions from the Virgin Mary, the Mother of God. Following is an excerpt from the book and is part of the message Mary gave for us all. I believe the message speaks to what you have read so far.

"The World stands in great danger during these days of great loss. The lack of love of God and each other as children of God has brought about the possible destruction of many. Our Lord is not happy with the behavior of his children..."

"I have seen mankind bring suffering upon itself because of lack of respect and kindness for each other and because of the desire for power, control, and material things. Men no longer want to feel or tolerate the pain they have brought upon themselves, so they fill their bodies with substances that can deceive their souls and make their minds believe all is well." [Prozac, Zoloft, Ritalin...

my words]

" I ask today of those who are praying for my work that you especially pray for those who control the world, because as they have been put in positions of power, they have left God's mandates and have placed themselves as gods over people. They set up their own mandates and are leading people astray and toward perdition and destruction. Pray my children that these men and women may not be successful in their attempts to rule not only the body of people, but their minds and spirits, for surely they will drive the world to destruction and chaos..."

The pharmaceutical companies are all but in control of the health of the United States and are seeking world domination. Many clearly see school shootings and workplace shootings as the result of medications. The Citizens Commission on Human Rights International has reported the link of many of our current school shootings and murders such as Columbine High School to the use of pyschotropic drugs. In a letter from the Citizens Commission on Human Rights International, they quote from an article on the front page of the Philadelphia News Observer. "Bruce Wiseman was quoted as saying, 'This has truly become one of the most dangerous and insidious situations facing American life—the fraudulent labeling and drugging of millions of our nation's youth with psychiatric mind altering drugs—a circumstance that has caused a corresponding increase in acts of violence in our schools".

Remember Mary's plea—"Pray my children that these

men and women may not be successful in their attempts to rule not only the body of people, but their minds and spirits…" Surely you must believe that drugs can control our bodies, minds and spirits. The idea that we should rely on drugs for every ailment, that drugs are the miracles and salvation from sickness and disease is a lie. A lie that we must shed light on before it is too late! Adolf Hitler said, "Tell a lie, tell if often enough, and people will believe it".

W.W.J.D.?

The people of the world are trying to take refuge and mask their pain with devices that numb the pain and the senses that mask or alter reality. Those things that put up a temporary wall of happiness. Drugs are the greatest of these. Yes, street drugs, but also non-prescription drugs or over the counter medications, alcohol and prescription medications. Can having pain exist in our lives possibly be beneficial? Shedding a positive light on pain for a moment let me suggest that it can be good when viewed from a different aspect. That is—as a warning of a greater problem. The pain itself is not the problem, just an indicator. All too often, this indicator is circumvented or shut off and the real problem still remains. Pain can be viewed positively in another way. As a catalyst that spur human beings to go beyond our comfort zones and helps our fellow man that is in need. Let me explain.

I am part of a medical missionary team that travels to

Mexico annually providing care to the poor families in some remote mountain villages. The multi disciplinary team consists of chiropractors, medical doctors, dentists, pharmacists, and nurses, support staff, workers and translators. A Catholic parish in Austin, Texas sponsors the mission. While on one of the missions, Bishop John McCarthy from Austin visited one of the ranchos to see the people and observe the work we were doing. While there, he gave a mass for one of the small towns, Los Lirios. This was quite a wonderful treat for the people who don't always have a priest available to them. To have the American Bishop was a special honor.

During the mass, the Bishop spoke specifically about pain and how it affects us all. As I reflect his words, (it was over three years ago so I may have to ask his forgiveness on quoting him), he posed a question to us. He said to ask ourselves, "What is God trying to teach me?" He said that pain holds a lesson for all of us if we will but ask the question, hear the answers and truly listen. The blessing in pain is that it seems to remind us of our fellow man, it reminds us of Jesus' suffering on the cross, to cleanse us of the pain of our sin. Each of our fellow humans are our responsibility just as we are Jesus' responsibility.

If our neighbors are in pain, our duty demands that we care for them. To me, this is the only reason to look at pain positively to show us how to care for each other. We must look, however, beyond the person's immediate pain to the condition or cause of the pain so that they can truly be healed. We all need to answer the question, "How can we fulfill our requirement on this earth to minister to others and love one another?" I believe ministering to others by teaching them how to use God's natural supplements is one powerful way to promote healing of the planet and fulfill our responsibility.

Pain in our bodies can be viewed as synonymous with pain in society and the world. Not only should we attempt to heal the world's pain, but realize that the pain itself is only a symptom of deeper-rooted problems. The cause of the symptoms of a painful world must be found and treated. Just as I teach patients in my practice, treating the symptoms only gives an individual temporary relief, but isn't long lasting. The cause must be found and eliminated for true healing to take place.

To heal a person, we must truly get to the root of the difficulty and eliminate it. Then we can restore health or homeostasis (balance) to the body. The overall pain the world feels must not only be dealt with on an individual level, but also on a collective level. But before we can heal the world, we must heal ourselves and our families. Before you can really love another, you must first truly love yourself. We must delve into the heart of the difficulties. The world is in pain not only from their individual bodily aches and pains, but from racism, corruption, greed, immorality, prejudice, death, violence, etc. Our spirits must be healed because we are spiritual beings. As hard as this may be for some people to believe, it means we are all exactly alike in our essence. The outward appearance is only a nice piece of camouflage. It is purely an illusion of the being internal. Our faces, languages, styles, and religious beliefs are only important on a very superficial level on this plane of existence.

Many perceived barriers and obstacles can be crossed when we attempt to come to the aid of a person in need. Have you ever noticed that when a life is in danger, no one asks or cares whether the person being saved or the rescuer is black, white, Jewish, Catholic, American, Russian, tall, short, speaks our language or not. What is important is survival. We can cross these same perceived barriers anytime we so choose. It doesn't only have to occur in times of crisis. What better way to cross these barriers than to look after the daily health of a person. Nutritional supplements, herbs, magnets, these things can all be barrier busters that say I am interested in you and your health. You will be healthier, happier, and more productive. Have you ever noticed that happy people generally get along with everyone? Feeding the internal health of a person will allow their spirit to manifest to its fullest glory. Allowing the use of medications only serves to extinguish this God given light. What is your vision for yourself? What is your vision for the world?

"You must be the change you wish to see in the world!"

-Mahatma Gandi

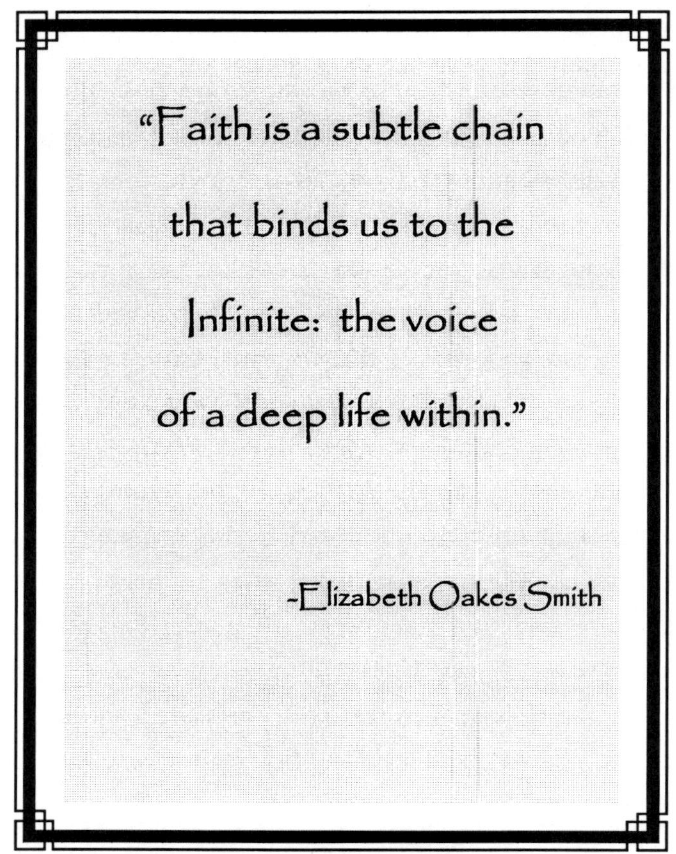
"Faith is a subtle chain
that binds us to the
Infinite: the voice
of a deep life within."
-Elizabeth Oakes Smith

Chapter 17

The Power of a Testimonial

Faith healing, spontaneous healing, chiropractic healing, herbal, vitamin, and mineral healing, essential oils magnets and more. All are real, all having power and truth. We are miracles of God and can use His power, our power and all the natural substances of the earth to heal. We can beckon the powers of the universe, use the electrical energy fields of our bodies and the cosmos to heal. We but need to seek the answers, believe, truly believe in the outcome and have faith and trust that our wishes for healing will come true. Remember—God wants us to be healthy!

"Beloved, I pray that you may prosper in all things and be in health, just as your soul prospers".

-III John 2

Know with certainty that natural healing pathways are real, efficacious, and powerful. Remember we are created in God's own image, therefore, we are pure energy, pure spirit. We have been given a physical form to temporarily house our spirit. We have been given a world to inhabit while we are in this form. This planet is full of abundance for us. God would not create beings in His likeness only to abandon them in a desolate environment with no hope for health and ultimate performance. We have only begun to understand the benefits this world holds for us. Remember that health comes from above, down to us, inside of us and then emanates out of us. We become empowered by hearing and knowing the truth. Engage not just your logical, conscious mind, but tap into your spirit, your intuitive and innate resources that will allow you to understand and know the truth when it is presented to you.

Read the truth about what the human body is capable of when given the correct means of healing. Read the following testimonies and know there is hope, there is healing and there is health in using the nutrients, the plants, the fruits that God created for our health and vitality. These stories are from ordinary people like you and I, but who had extraordinary faith, wisdom and desire to heal through natural means.

"I was not looking for chiropractic care when I met Dr. Barrett four months ago. I had already chosen to accept the belief that my chronic, life long back problems were just that-chronic and life long."

"I have suffered from debilitating back pain since childhood. While still a baby, my parents were told that I was born with a weak spine, but that it would 'strengthen and correct itself'".

"By the time I first visited a chiropractor at age 21, I had already injured and traumatized my back more than most other kids I knew. I missed many days of school due to pain so severe that it was impossible to stand or walk. As a young adult, I was missing time at work, and at risk of losing my job."

"I have received chiropractic care intermittently for

20 years. But I only initiated it when my back pain would flare up. Yes, the adjustments helped, but I felt detached from the healer's methods, never really understanding the chiropractic philosophy, and I was never shown how to aid in my own healing."

"Dr. Barrett made a big impression on me the first time I heard him talk. He explained the sources of health and the cause of dis-ease. When I visited his clinic, he brought me, the patient, into the healing process. Not just as an injured, suffering body, but as a whole person who's body and *mind are healthier when the central nervous systems is functioning properly."*

"In the past, I lived with restrictions and caution. Dr. Barrett encouraged me to look at positive outcomes, to set goals, to visualize myself pain free and to trust that he could get me there if we worked on it together.*"*

"For two years before meeting Dr. Barrett, I was overmedicated with prescription drugs, most of them swallowed just to mask the side effects of another. I was depressed, disheartened and confused over what really was wrong with me. If the drugs are supposed to help me, I wondered, why do I feel so lousy?"

"Dr. Barrett opened my mind to the possibility that chiropractic healing might be able to target my ailments. He also convinced me that the drugs were doing me far more harm than good. He urged me to hang on to my goals while I met with disdain from medical doctors for giving up my medications."

"Four months later, thanks to Dr. Barrett's healing methods, I live free of chronic headaches, sore joints, neck, shoulder, back and hip pain. My flexibility has improved greatly, and I enjoy activities like golf and gardening much more now."

"Dr. Barrett's advice on vitamin and herbal supplements has helped ease my insomnia, mood swings and fatigue, naturally and safely."

"I no longer push myself through the day feeling empty and unenthused. Now I have a positive outlook and am motivated to pursue even more avenues to wellness."

"I thank God for guiding me to Dr. Barrett. And I thank Dr. Barrett for his using his gift of healing with integrity and caring concern."

-Deborah Da Silva

✝ ✝ ✝

"Hi, my name is Pam Doolittle and I am a Manager with, a nutrition company. My product testimony starts in December 1996 with the diagnosis of the return of my hyperthyroid. The normal range is 4-12. My count was 17.5. I started using some thyroid products at that time. When I finally got to the specialist in May, the count had gone down to 15.5, which to me meant I was using some of the right products, just not enough."

"With my history and prior use of a medication which, by the way, caused me to gain thirty pounds in five months back in 1994, the doctor said we needed to schedule a procedure where I would be given some radioactive

iodine. This would supposedly go to the thyroid and destroy the overactive part, and then you end up taking a synthetic thyroid for the rest of your life. I told him I would prefer to take my herbs and do another blood test. He hesitated, but agreed."

"With the help of an herbalist friend of mine, I began a 'treatment' which included the thyroid products and several others. To get to the point, my count just six weeks later was 11.3. We were all elated. The doctor asked me, 'Why am I here?' I replied that he was supposed to learn about these nutritional products and be able to give his other patients alternatives to taking medication, radioactive iodine or surgery. I have had many other great results with these products and I invite you all to experience the same. I certainly am convinced that if we feed our body right, the body will heal itself. Thank you!"

"I am a 48 year old man who hasn't been real careful with his body. I have never been sickly, but with my sinuses acting up a lot and five degenerative discs in my spine, I went through a period of five or so years when I had severe headaches."

"During one particular bad stretch, I had a severe headache for four days. Someone recommended I try feverfew. I was willing to try anything at that point. To my amazement, the headache ended that day. I continued

to take about four a day for the next three months."

"I had been taking about 150 mg. of ibuprofen for months previous to trying the herb. That was about three years ago and I haven't had any ibuprofen since. I now regularly take feverfew and echinacea as well as having my back adjusted by the best, Dr. Barrett.

-Ray Martin

"It's difficult to put one's life's philosophy into one short paragraph, but I'll try. I've always believed in using holistic medicine over putting chemical pharmaceuticals into by body. It only makes sense. These beliefs stem from my rural grandmother who always had a home remedy for whatever ailed us, usually something she'd read in the Farmer's Almanac. Maybe because in her days there was no such things as 24 hour drug stores eager to sell their wares any time of the day or night, and you had to just make due with what God put on the earth around us to use. I remember her using the bud of an onion, warmed and placed gently into the ear to remedy the worst childhood earache. Molasses and ginger would always soothe a sore throat and cough and cumin was just plain good for your digestive system, like cranberry juice was to a urinary infection. Scientific evidence I can't offer you, but I can tell you from experience these potions worked their magic and soothed our ailments. To this day, my grandmother, age 91 lives without any medi-

cations of any kind and has a drug free body. She is the proof, natural health is the way to go."

-Heather Langlais

"Chiropractic care, herbs and natural vitamins have been a way of life for me for many years. However, a freak accident caused me to believe in natural remedies more than ever before. While decorating a new home, I had a bad fall, resulting in months of medical care and yet there was no relief for the pain. I felt drugged all the time. A friend suggested I try some herbal products from a company she was associated with. Incredibly, after using only one of the products just one time, I woke up the next day without any pain. Needless to say, the experience made a real believer out of me and in the future I will always consider natural remedies first."

-Pat Kushnir

As the final steps were being taken to finish this book, a tragic incident involving a friend of mine occurred. His story and the power of prayer are so powerful that I felt it needed to be included. The words are his own and truly they deliver the message that we all can be Healed by Morning. This is Dave's story:

As Mark Twain once said, "the reports of my death

have been greatly exaggerated!" But in all seriousness, I owe my life to all of my friends and loved ones here in the Sugar Land community. The past couple of weeks have been full of so many different emotions. Emotions of fear overcome by joy... emotions of laughter overcome by tears. But the one emotion that I continue to hold true, is that of thankfulness and praise to God for sparing my life and watching over my family.

As an active member of the National Exchange Club, my family and I were in Phoenix to participate in the National Convention. We were joined there by about two thousand "Exchangites" from throughout the country, including a number of fellow club members from Sugar Land and Fort Bend. On Saturday, July 15th, our family planned to go horseback riding, so I did not have enough time for my regular workout. So instead, I got out of bed, grabbed the newspaper from the door, and strolled down to the pool at 6:30 a.m., to relax a bit, read the paper and then join my family.

Well, these well-thought-out plans were not meant to be, and what followed was a series of miracles and the response to thousands of prayers.

I remember setting my newspaper down at a poolside table. I even remember walking into the pool and floating around in a state of relaxation. But the next several hours are a period of time that I will never remember, except by listening to the stories of those involved. For some reason, I was rendered unconscious and sank to the bottom of the pool. No one knows exactly how long I was under water, but the police say that there is a ten-minute period of time from when folks at the hotel saw me on the surface, and when I was pulled from the pool. The doctors say that brain damage due to the lack of oxygen starts in the two- to three-minute range, and is pretty intense at four minutes. The fact that I still have all of my faculties is, in itself, a miracle.

Based on police reports, at 7:25 a.m., some of the hotel guests saw me from a balcony and started banging on doors for the people to call 911 and started yelling to maintenance staff about a man at the bottom of the pool. Unfortunately, the first staff member could not speak English, nor could he swim. However, he quickly got two other staff members to help pull me out of the pool.

Meanwhile, a maintenance worker named Pat Flores was taking her cigarette break. But instead of taking her break at her usual spot, she said that there was something calling her to get into a golf cart, drive one-half mile away and have a cigarette at the very pool where I was swimming. So here is Pat tucked away near the service elevator smoking a cigarette, when she hears all of the commotion. The importance of Pat to this story is that she is the only one present who knows CPR. (In fact, I was the fourth person to whom she has administered CPR; however, I was the first of these four to survive!)

At this point in time, I had no heart beat, no pulse, no breathing, lungs full of water, non-responsive eyes, and paralyzed from the neck down. In effect, I was dead.

However, the miracles continued as the first 911 call was placed. Simply by coincidence, a Phoenix police car was at the front entrance of the hotel. So, in less than a couple of minutes, additional EMS support was on hand to support Ms. Flores. Shortly thereafter, the Phoenix Fire Department and ambulance arrived to help stabilize me and start placing a tracheotomy tube down my nose and throat.

So here I am unconscious, and as they are preparing me for the ambulance trip, the police officer asks those standing around if anyone knows who I am to notify family members. Ironically, one of the first people to spot me from the balcony was a great friend whom I see quite often. However, due to the lack of oxygen and intake of water, my face was so blue and swollen, even my good friend Bill Deason did not recognize me. (In fact, later at the hospital the police had to take a second look at my driver's license and still were not sure they had informed the right family.)

Fortunately, the police discovered that I had a room key in the pocket of my bathing suit. It was the kind of key with the magnetic strip and no room numbers for security purposes. So, for the next twenty minutes, the police officers went floor-by-floor and room-to-room in an attempt to get a green entry light. Eventually, they found the right room (on the fourth floor) and as Kathy answered the door, the stone-faced officer asked Kathy a question that she will never forget: "When was the last time that you saw your husband?" You can imagine the feeling of despair that quickly fell over my family as the officer continued by stating that there had been an accident in the pool, and that their husband and father was taking only a few, faint breaths as the ambulance drove off.

Before leaving for the hospital, Kathy asked that hotel security call down to the Child Abuse Prevention (CAP) breakfast that was underway to locate Brenda Robinson, a good friend and president of our local Sugar Land Exchange Club. After a few minutes of no success in locating her, Whitney, our 13-year-old daughter, said "Forget it, I'll get her!" Whitney sprinted to the banquet hall and found some fellow Sugar Land and Fort Bend Exchange Club members and told them what had happened. In a matter of minutes, Kathy and Whitney were at the front of the hotel in a van loaded with Sugar Land friends, ready to go to the hospital.

Fortunately, it was at this moment that the power of prayer started. As the word got to the head table at the CAP breakfast, a moment of silence and prayer was offered for my safety. In fact, about two thousand of my closest friends (the bond of Exchange is very strong!) started to pray for my health and safety. Many of these people did not have any information on the current situation, but from the initial reports, the prognosis did not look good.

Meanwhile, back at the hospital, Kathy and all of our

great friends from Sugar Land arrived to some somber news. I was on life support, had a ventilator breathing for me and still paralyzed from the neck down. An MRI revealed that my brain was swollen and my eyes were non-responsive and floating from side to side. Kathy was quickly assigned a counselor to help in making final arrangements, to help in communicating with other family members and to ease the doctor's words of "all we can do is pray at this point." In fact, the hospital quickly decided that I needed to be Life Flighted to a second hospital, one that was better suited for the neurological trauma that the doctors envisioned.

Prior to being Life Flighted, two extremely important things involved in my recovery took place. The first event was all of our Sugar Land and Fort Bend Exchange Club friends standing in the hospital parking lot (remember you can't use cell phones in the hospital) calling home to inform people of what had happened. From what I understand, the number of friends and neighbors, fellow members of Exchange, St. Laurence parishioners and others who came together in prayer was unlike anything I could believe. For this support, I am eternally grateful.

The second event of importance was that Kathy was asked if she wanted to see me (which may have been the last time alive) before the Life Flight. It took a lot of emotional and spiritual energy, with the support of our great friend Brenda, for Kathy to see me. When Kathy came into the trauma center, she had little hope of my recovery and, in fact, was already thinking of things such as how I would miss walking Whitney and Jacquelyn down the aisle on their wedding days, how I would miss standing on the sidelines and cheering for our daughters' soccer games, etc. According to Kathy, she remembers a number of people working frantically on me, but the rest seemed like a blur as she quickly became fixated on my face. At this point in time, I was still unconscious, moving my head from side-to-side, yet my eyes were still rolling back in my head. Kathy walked up and very quietly whispered through her tears, "You are such a fighter in business... you are such a fighter in the community... don't stop fighting now." Although I have no recollection of these words, I immediately stopped moving my head from side-to-side, and started to stare in the direction of her voice. I also started to kick my once-paralyzed legs for the first time.

I firmly believe that the reason that I am alive today is a direct result of the intense power of prayer that took place within minutes of being found at the bottom of the pool.

I have truly felt the power of prayer from our community at a level that I have never experienced before, and I owe you my life. According to all of the Phoenix doctors, police, and EMS technicians, I should not have lived through the drowning. For this, I want to thank all of you who prayed for me.

Can Chiropractic heal? Can nutritional supplements heal? Can prayer heal? Absolutely! It is possible to experience, be witness to and be the affect of any number of natural healing methods. We don't have to live lives shackled to a cabinet full of medicine, to be forever dependent upon pharmaceuticals to sustain us and maintain us.

There can be life without drugs! We don't have to exist the way this cartoon depicts, but sadly it is reflective of the world today. Each one of us is free to make choices; you decide is this the life you envision for yourself and your family?

What would Jesus do? Or Mohammed, Buddha, or the higher power you believe in?

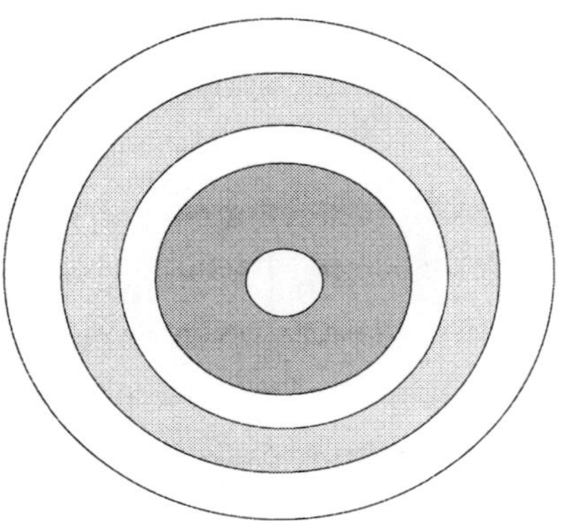

Now that you have finished the book and gained some additional insight, look at the target again. Reevaluate what you think and believe. I hope that I have awakened or stirred some fire in you to become healthier and to help others achieve health. I hope I have elevated your awareness! Now put a mark on this target and compare it with the original. Where are you now? Has your purpose changed? Are you more motivated to share natural healing with others? Can you believe that God has a plan for us to be healthy and, in fact, programmed us for perfect health? Do you believe that you are capable of changing, not only your health, but also elevating the health of the planet? Can you see that you are a miracle from God, as is each and every human being? Can you see your responsibility to mankind? It is an awesome responsibility to be our brother's keeper but one that you are completely capable of. Do not be afraid to share natural healing with every human being, every one you meet, everyone God brings into your life! The health of the planet depends on you. The alternative is death and destruction. Dream of a life worth living, live a life of dreams. Be the guide for others to follow.

Dream Dreams

Dreams come and go in our lives.
Far more die than come to reality.
What is it in us that allows us to let go of visions that could
create new and beautiful worlds?
Why do we so easily give in to barriers?
Why do we let ourselves conform and
be satisfied with what is?
Reaching out to a dream can be risky.
It can involve hardships that our imaginations never knew.
Our comfortableness can so easily be disturbed.
But, what beauty can be experienced as we
accept the challenge of a dream!
What a precious feeling to be supported,
to have others say you can do it, we can do it together.
Nothing is beyond our reach if we reach out together, if we
reach out with all the confidence we have, if we are willing to
persevere even in difficult
times and if we rejoice with every small step
forward, if we dream
beautiful dreams that will transform our lives, our world.
Nothing is impossible if we put aside our careful ways, if we
build our dreams with faith—faith in ourselves, faith in our
sisters and brothers, and above all,
faith in our Lord God with whom all things are possible.

-Author Unknown

Parting Thoughts

"Be watchful, stand firm in
your faith, be courageous,
be strong.
Let all that you do
be done in love."

-I Corinthians 16:13

Many times I had asked the questions, "Why am I writing this book?" "Who will read it?" "Will those who read it listen, or ignore the truth as so many do?" From the moment I started this project, it seemed as though I was caught up in a wild river that consumed me and carried me on and on.

Through much of this writing, I have felt a great sense of urgency to get the book together and published for people to read. Urgency not from the stand point of being tired of the writing, but that there was little time and every day wasted or everyday it wasn't in someone's hands, was another day that someone's life might be lost. You see, I fully expect that this book will save a life, perhaps many. Not that this book is perfect or that I am a wonderfully gifted writer, but this book is a creation of God.

I feel as though I was driven to continue the work even when problems arose, even when it took me away from my personal life or my work of chiropractic. It has consumed much of my time, life, thoughts and focus. Many nights were spent awakening at 2:00 or 4:00 in the morning, wide-awake with thoughts, passages, or pages worth of writing bursting out of my subconscious needing to be written down. All these thoughts couldn't be my own some were being given to me from a higher power. At least this is my perception. Many times I would not even be working on the book for days or perhaps weeks when thoughts and sentences and paragraphs would come rushing to me and with a definite sense of immediacy. I would have to stop what I was doing or arise from bed and write.

So many times I felt that the project was taking too long and interrupting too much of my existence. So many problems continually arose. On three separate occasions the book was almost lost through computer failures. Thank God for the written word and paper! It slowed me down. Created extra work for those who were entering the work into the computer, it retarded the process. Much anxiety, frustration, and anger was created. I felt like giving up several times. But the overwhelming feeling from my innate was that it was a worthwhile piece, that it would touch lives and needed to be completed. I needed to finish this because I don't like unfinished work, but beyond that, society needs to hear the words that have been shared here. Human beings need to have repetition in their lives to fully grasp an idea, new thought, new routine, new concepts, new languages, and new ways of doing things. The more we all keep vigilant and empower ourselves with reason and truth, then the greater chance we have of freedom from sickness, disease and a life of dependency on the toxic medications of the pharmaceutical world that seeks to keep us shackled to them.

As others have said before, knowledge is power, and the truth shall set you free. Destinies can be often confusing and purpose frequently never found:

I hope to open your heart, mind and soul to truth, to viewing the world from a new point of view. And to give support, and inspiration to those who already can see through the fog.

My wish is that you will experience excellence in your life, that much success, happiness and health will be part of your physical existence on this planet. And that you will empower others to experience the same.

As my good friend Dr. Bellamy, writes in his book, The 12 Secrets for Manifesting Your Vision, Inspiration & Purpose:

"Persevere in your meaningful purpose with principled conceptualization, holding your vision continuously before you, with your calling within you, your feeling drawing you, your grand plan before you, your action expressed by you, with energy on your matter at hand, and gratitude for all that is, was, and will be."

Be the light for another's darkness! Health and healing to you and yours,

Dr. R. F. Barrett, D.C.

"I slept and dreamt that life was joy, I awoke and saw that life was service.

I acted and behold, service was joy."

-Rabindranath Tagore

Lord God you are my creator. I love you.

I am part of you, therefore,
I cannot fail because you cannot fail.

I am capable of everything. Ultimate health,
happiness and success because I am part of
you, and you are completely capable.

Every good wish I have, I can have,
because you wish it for me.

I will not linger in darkness and doubt,
because the spirit of your light
illuminates my way.
You are in me and I am one with you.

Together we can accomplish miracles.

-R.F. Barrett, D.C.

About The Author...

Education and Professional Credentials

- Doctorate Degree from Cleveland Chiropractic College in Kansas City, Missouri
- Bachelor of Science in Nutrition from Park College, Parkville, Missouri
- Board Certification:
  National Board of Chiropractic Examiners
  Texas Board of Chiropractic Examiners

Awards

- Cleveland Chiropractic College—Clinic Service Award in recognition of dedicated commitment and service to patients.
- Certificate of Appreciation for Outstanding Service to Cleveland Chiropractic College.
- Recognized and Published in National Deans List for Academic Excellence.
- Recipient of the Doctor Martha Metz Memorial Scholarship and the Doctor Robert Gerred Memorial Scholarship.
- Listed in the 1996 and 1997 National Directory of Who's Who in Leading Professionals and Executives
- Listed in the 1998 and 1999 American Directory of Who's Who in Executive and Businesses as an honored professional.

- Listed in Strathmore's 1999 and 2000 Who's Who for Leadership and Achievement.
- Recipient of the Cystic Fibrosis Foundation's, "Houston's Singular Best" Award given for professional excellence and charitable and civic contributions to the Houston area.

Military Experience

- Served in the armed forces for 7 years as a Sea Bee and honorably discharged from the U.S. Navy.

Instructor

- Certified American Red Cross Instructor for the *"Protect Your Back"* program.

Professional Associations

- Member of:

  International Chiropractic Association
  Texas Chiropractic Association
  World Chiropractic Alliance
  Foundation for Chiropractic Education and Research
  Ft. Bend Chamber of Commerce
  Knights of Columbus
  Ft. Bend Sports Chiropractic Team
  Ft. Bend YMCA-Board of Directors
  and Committee Member
  American Holistic Health Association

Mission Work

- Involved in yearly medical missions to Mexico since 1995 with an interdisciplinary team providing chiropractic care to the under privileged.

Published

- Author of "Dare to Break Through the Pain; *A Guide to Eliminating Back & Neck Pain Naturally Without Drugs or Surgery!"*
- Contributing writer to "A Texas Christmas".
- Published in the Houston Business Journal.
- Contributing writer to Countryside magazine.

- Contributing column writer to El Dia newspaper.
- Contributing writer to Healthy Spirit magazine.

Public Speaker

Dr. Barrett lectures, speaks and gives workshops on a variety of health topics such as:

- Back Safety
- Injury Prevention
- Stress
- Headaches
- Carpal Tunnel
- Attention Deficit Disorder
- Nutrition

He also speaks on medical missionary work. Some of Dr. Barrett's appearances have been:

- Houston Community College
- Tenneco Marathon
- The Methodist Health Care Houston Marathon Health and Fitness Expo
- U.S. Government
- U. S. Postal Office
- Continuing education program for Fort Bend County League of LVN's

Dr. Barrett also provides back safety, human performance and ergonomic evaluations in the work place for entities such as:

- Missouri City Fire Department
- Sugar Land Fire Department

Community Service

His office sponsors annual charitable events including school supply, food and toy drives. Donations are given to the East Fort Bend Human Needs Ministry Food Pantry, and United Way. Dr. Barrett volunteers his services as part of the Ft. Bend Sports Chiropractic Team providing chiropractic care to the rodeo cowboys at the Ft. Bend County Fair and Rodeo. He has also been a sponsor for the Ft. Bend Polo Cup benefiting the YMCA Partners of Youth and a charter sponsor for the Boy Scout Rangers.

Dr. Barrett has a passion for sharing natural healing with others and is always available for lectures.

To contact Dr. Barrett for seminars, lectures or consultations or for further information, he may be reached via...

Mail: **Dr. Richard F. Barrett, B.S.,D.C.**
2853 Dulles Avenue
Missouri City, TX 77459

Phone: **281-499-4810**
Toll Free: **866-222-HEAL (4325)**
Fax: **281-499-3005**

Website: **www.dr-barrett.com**
www.healedbymorning.com

E-Mail: **drrfb@flash.net**

If this book has touched your life in some way, please share your story with us.

Resources and References

Library of Health Complete Guide to Prevention and Cure of Disease, Edited by B. Frank Scholl, Ph. G.M.D. , Historical Publishing Company, Philadelphia, PA
Copyright 1916

The New Strong's Exhaustive Concordance of the Bible, James Strong, L.L.D., S.T.D., Thomas Nelson Publishers, Nashville, Atlanta, London, Vancouver, Copyright 1990

Commitment to Excellence Celebrating Excellence, Inc., Copyright 1993

365 TAO Daily Meditations, Deng Ming-Dao Harper, San Francisco, Copyright 1992

The Graduate and the Master, Paul Turnbull, Copyright 1997

Proverbs Maxims and Phrases of All Ages, Compiled by Robert Christy, P. Putnam's Sons, The Knickerbocker Press New York, Copyright 1888

The Bible Cure, Reginal Cherry, M. D., Published by Creation House, Strang Communications Company
Lake Mary, FL, Copyright 1998

The N. I. V. Study Bible, Zondervan Publishing House, Grand Rapids, MI, Copyright 1995

Scientology 0-8 The Book of Basics, Ron Hubbard
Bridge Publications, Los Angeles, CA, Copyright 1988

The Healing Power of Herbs, Michael T. Murray
Prima Publishing, Copyright 1992

The Science of Personal Achievement, The 17 Universal Principles of Success, Napolean Hill, Produced by Nightengale Conant, Niles, IL, Copyright

Six Attitudes for Winners, Norman Vincent Peale
Tyndale House Publishers, Incorporated, Wheaton, IL,Copyright 1989

It's All Within Your Reach, How to Live Your Dreams, Nightengale Conant, Chicago, IL, Copyright

A Better Way to Live, Og Mandino, Bantam Books,
New York, Copyright 1990

Textbook of Medical Physiology, Arthur C. Guyton, M. D., B. Saunders Company, Philadelphia, PA, Copyright 1986, 7th Edition

For the Soul of the Family, Thomas Petrisko. Queenship Publishing, Santa Barbara, CA, Copyright 1996

Mother Teresa No Greater Love, New World Library, Novato, CA, Copyright 1989

Other Sources:
Citizens Commission on Human Rights International, White Paper, 6362 Hollywood Blvd., Suite B, Los Angeles, CA 90028, 213-467-4242

Health Report, David Singer Enterprises, 1130 Cleveland Street, Suite 210, Clearwater, FL 33755, 1-800-326-1797

Health Watch, 2950 N. Dobson Road #1, Chandler, AZ 85224, 602-732-9313

Internet:

HTTP://WEB.raex.com/~COLOMBO/PROZAC 1.HTM

HTTP://WEB.raex.com/~COLOMBO/PROZAC 2.HTM

Drug-Free America Cartoon, Reprinted with permission of Cartoonists & Writers Syndicate and Signe, 67 Riverside Dr., N.Y, N.Y., 10024

Order Form...

Copy this order form and mail to:

Barrett Chiropractic Clinic
2853 Dulles Avenue, Missouri City, TX 77459

Ship To:
Name____
Address______________________________________
City, State, Zip _________________________________
Phone ( )_____________________________________
or Call your order to: **281-499-4810** or fax to: **281-499-3005**

$19.95 per book x quantity ______ = Sub-total __________
(8.25% in Texas) Sales Tax__________
($4 first book and $2 each additional book) Shipping __________
Total ____________

I would also like to order **Dare To Break Through the Pain, A Guide to Eliminating Back & Neck Pain Naturally Without Drugs or Surgery!**

$12.95 per book x quantity ______ = Sub-total _________
(8.25% in Texas) Sales Tax ________
($4 first book and $2 each additional book) Shipping ________
Total ___________

Method of Payment: Check Visa Master Card Discover

Name on card ____________________________________
Card Number ____________________________________
Expiration Date __________________________________

Thank you for your order! We will deliver immediately.

This book is available at a special discount when ordered in bulk quantities. Contact Dream Weaver Press toll free at **866-222-4325**

✤*Merci Beaucoup*✤ ✤*Tack Koszonom*✤

✤*Ashante*✤

✤*Gracias*✤ ✤*Goszaimasu*✤

✤*Thanks*✤

✤*Tante Grazie*✤ ✤*Mahalo*✤

✤*Shukran*✤

✤*Diolch*✤ ✤*Takke*✤

✤*Arigato*✤

✤*Tussen Tack*✤ ✤*Spieseba*✤